Off the Charts Law Summaries

Off the Charts Law Summaries

An All-In-One Graphic Outline of the 1L Law School Courses

Julie Schechter

CAROLINA ACADEMIC PRESS

Durham, North Carolina

Library of Congress Cataloging-in-Publication Data

Schechter, Julie F., author.
  Off the charts law summaries : an all-in-one graphic outline of the 1L law school
courses / Julie Schechter.
    pages cm
  ISBN 978-1-61163-260-6 (alk. paper)
  1. Law--United States--Outlines, syllabi, etc. I. Title.
  KF388.S34 2014
  349.7302'02--dc23   2013048927

Carolina Academic Press
700 Kent Street
Durham, North Carolina 27701
Telephone (919) 489-7486
Fax (919) 493-5668
www.cap-press.com

Printed in the United States of America
2017 Printing

To my incredible parents.
Thank you for your endless love and support.

Contents

About the Author and Editor

Julie Schechter graduated from the University of Maryland, College Park with a degree in Criminology & Criminal Justice and went on to receive her Juris Doctor from Brooklyn Law School. Ms. Schechter is a practicing attorney admitted to practice law in the state and federal courts of New York. Since graduating from law school, she has been working as an attorney at Schechter & Brucker, P.C., a boutique real estate law firm that focuses on Cooperative and Condominium Law in the New York metropolitan area, and also tutoring law students in regular coursework throughout the semester. As a law student, Ms. Schechter created charts to help her study because through charts she found she was able to present the voluminous, complex material in a simple, straightforward format. Ms. Schechter continues to use those charts to help the students she tutors and has created this book to help a wider range of students gain a comprehensive understanding of the five subjects taught during the first year of law school and tested on the Multistate portion of the bar exam.

Monica E. Kipiniak is an attorney admitted to practice law in the state and federal courts of New York and New Jersey. She maintains a private practice in Brooklyn, New York, and has been working with law students for close to 20 years. Ms. Kipiniak provides private tutoring for students requiring individual assistance in their preparation for law school and the bar exams. Ms. Kipiniak primarily prepares students for the New York and New Jersey bar examinations, but has also assisted individuals taking bar exams in Texas, Massachusetts, Connecticut, Pennsylvania, Minnesota, Arkansas and California. She has lectured at various law schools throughout New York state on preparing and taking the bar exam, and has been responsible for editing and creating bar exam preparation materials. Beginning in the fall of 2014, she will begin teaching a bar preparation class at New York Law School.

Off the Charts Law Summaries

Civil Procedure

Federal Rules of Civil Procedure	The Federal Rules of Civil Procedure (FRCP) are regulations that specify procedures for civil legal suits within United States federal courts.

Summaries of Selected FRCP Provisions

Below are summaries of selected provisions of the FRCP, which are intended to be used as a quick reference.
Look to the actual FRCP for a more complete description of the law.

Rule	Title	Description
1	Scope & Purpose	These rules govern the procedure in all civil actions and proceedings in the United States district courts.
4	Summons	(a) Summons must name the court and the parties, be directed to the defendant, state the name and address of the plaintiff's attorney or plaintiff if unrepresented, state the time within which defendant must appear and defend, notify defendant that a failure to appear and defend will result in a default judgment, be signed by the clerk and bear the court's seal. (b) Court may permit a summons to be amended. (c) Summons must be served with a copy of the complaint by a person who is at least 18 years old and not a party. (d) Defendant can waive service.
7	Pleadings Allowed; Form of Motions	(a) Only pleadings allowed are: complaint, answer, reply to a counterclaim, third party complaint, third party answer, and answer to a cross claim. (b) Motions must be in writing, state with particularity the grounds for seeking the order, state relief sought and be signed according to Rule 11.
8	General Rules of Pleadings	(a) Pleadings must contain: basis for subject matter jurisdiction, nature of the claim, and a demand for the relief sought. (b) **Defenses; Admissions and Denials.** Defendant must state in short and plain terms its defenses to each claim and admit or deny the allegations asserted against it. • Defendant can plead that she is without knowledge or information sufficient to form a belief as to the truth of an allegation, which will be treated as a denial. • Denials must meet substance of complaint (if not, it is an ineffective denial and may constitute admission). • General Denials are when defendant denies every allegation of the entire complaint. Specific denials are denials to only certain allegations. • Failure to deny operates as an admission only when a responsive pleading is required and allegation is not denied. If responsive pleading is not required, allegation is considered denied or avoided. (c) **Affirmative defenses** include accord and satisfaction, arbitration and award, assumption of risk, contributory negligence, duress, estoppel, failure of consideration, fraud, illegality, injury by fellow servant, laches, license, payment, release, res judicata, statute of frauds, statute of limitations and waiver. (d) Each allegation must be simple, concise and direct, no technical form required.
10	Form of Pleadings	(a) Every pleading must contain: caption name of court, title of action which names all of the parties, file number, and type of pleading. (b) Separate claims and defenses need be limited to single sets of circumstances separately articulated in enumerated paragraphs. (c) May include exhibits.
11	Signing Pleadings and Motions; Representations to the Court; Sanctions	(a) <u>Signature</u>. Every pleading, written motion and other paper must have the signature of the party's attorney or that of a self-represented party, and the signer's address and telephone number. (b) <u>Representation</u>: If pleading, written motion or other paper is certified and not accurate, the party is subject to sanctions. By signing, signor is representing she conducted a reasonable inquiry into the matter, that the information she is presenting is true to the best of her knowledge, that all legal arguments are supported by existing law and all factual contentions are supported by evidence or likely to be supported by evidence after discovery. (c) <u>Sanctions</u>: may be imposed either following motion by a party or on the court's own initiative for any misrepresentation.

Summaries of Selected FRCP Provisions, *continued*

Rule	Title	Description
12	Defenses and Objections	(a) With exceptions, responses are usually required to be served within 21 days. (b) Responses should include denials, denials in the form of a declaration that an individual is without sufficient knowledge or information to form a belief, admissions and any affirmative defenses. The affirmative defenses of lack of jurisdiction, improper venue, failure to state a claim, failure to join a necessary party, or insufficiency of process or service of process can also be raised in a pre-answer motion to dismiss. Failure to raise the defense of lack of personal jurisdiction, improper venue, or insufficiency of process or service of process on a responding party's first responsive pleadings is a waiver of such defenses. (c) **Motion for Judgment on the Pleadings:** A party may move for summary judgment on the pleadings after an answer is filed, provided the motion does not delay a trial. (e) **Motion for a More Definite Statement:** A party may move for a more definite statement if a pleading is so vague or ambiguous that a party cannot reasonably prepare a response. (f) **Motion to Strike:** May be used to strike from any pleading an insufficient defense or any redundant, immaterial, impertinent or scandalous matter.
13	Counterclaim and Crossclaim	(a) **Compulsory Counterclaims:** A pleading *must* state as a counterclaim any claim that arises from the same transaction or occurrence as the claim against defendant that does not require a third party. (b) **Permissive Counterclaims:** A pleading *may* state any counterclaim that arises from an event unrelated to the matter on which the plaintiff's suit is based. (g) **Crossclaims:** a pleading may state as a crossclaim any claim by one party against a co-party when the same underlying facts will be litigated on the main claim and on the crossclaim. It must arise from the same transaction or occurrence as either the original complaint or counterclaim, or relate to property that is the subject matter of the transaction.
14	Third Party Practice	(a) **Impleader:** Preserves defendant's right to seek indemnity or contribution by allowing defendant to bring in a third party to whom liability may be shifted or shared with.
15	Amended and Supplemental Pleadings	(a) A party may amend its pleadings once without obtaining court permission provided that no responsive pleading has been served. Otherwise, permission to file an amended pleading must be obtained by written consent or by motion. (b) Amendments to pleadings after trial has begun will be allowed if evidence introduced changes the circumstances, and the opposing party does not object or explicitly consents. Where an opposing party does object to such amendment, the court may still permit the amendment where it is determined to be necessary to resolve the merits of the action. (c) Amendments of pleadings will relate back to the date of the original pleading provided that: • The statute of limitations has not run; OR • The claim or defense set forth in the amended pleading arose from the same conduct, transaction or occurrence as that of the original pleading; OR • Where the amendment is a substitution or addition of a party, the party being one who is aware or should have been aware she could be named as a defendant in the original action had it not been for the mistake as to the identity of the proper party. (d) **Supplemental Pleadings:** Set forth new facts that arise after the original pleading was filed. Supplemental pleadings are permitted upon motion of a party and order of the court.
18	Joinder	A party can add as many claims as it has against the opposing party.
19	Required Joinder of Parties	A party must be joined to an action, if feasible, if: (1) their absence prevents obtaining complete relief for the parties in litigation; OR (2) their absence prejudices the party not joined; OR (3) their absence prejudices parties already part of the litigation by threatening increased or inconsistent liability. If a court determines a party should be joined and the person cannot be joined the court may dismiss the suit.
20	Permissive Joinder of Parties	People may join or be joined to an action if: (1) there is an identical series of occurrences or transactions; AND (2) there is a common question of law or fact.

Summaries of Selected FRCP Provisions, *continued*

Rule	Title	Description
22	Interpleader	Special type of lawsuit brought by a custodian or stakeholder to resolve the potential conflict between two or more claimants over entitlement to an interest over which the custodian or stakeholder retains control.
23	Class Actions	(a) The following prerequisites are needed for one or more members of a class to sue or be sued on behalf of all members: (1) NUMEROSITY—class is so numerous that joinder of all members is impracticable, (2) COMMONALITY—there are questions of law or fact common to the class, (3) TYPICALITY—the claims or defenses of the representative parties are typical of the claims or defenses of the class, AND (4) ADEQUACY—the representative parties will fairly and adequately protect the interests of the class. (b) A class action will be maintained if: (1) there are numerous necessary parties and individual actions involving the class members pose a risk of either: (A) inconsistent or varying outcomes, OR (B) would dispose of or impair the interests of the other members, OR (2) Injunctive or declaratory relief is appropriate for a class as a whole, OR (3) Common question of fact or law predominate any questions affecting only individual members, and a class action is a superior method of adjudication (catch-all). (c) Notice to all class members of the pending litigation is required in suits involving a common question of fact or law.
24	Intervention	(a) **Intervention By Right**: does not require court permission. On timely motion, the court must allow anyone to intervene who has a legal right or interest in the subject of the action. (b) **Permissive Intervention**: a party may seek permission to intervene either when a statute grants a conditional right to intervene, OR when the applicant's claim or defense shares a common question of law or fact with the existing suit.
26	Duty to Disclose; Discovery	(a) A party must, without awaiting discovery request, provide to the opposing party within 14 days after the meeting of the parties: (1) the identity and location of each person who the disclosing party plans to use at trial, (2) a copy or description of all documents and tangible things that the party plans on using at trial, (3) a computation of damages claimed by the disclosing party, AND (4) The contents of any insurance agreement under which insurer will be liable to satisfy any judgment that may result. • **Expert Testimony**: the identity and qualifications, the expert's report, opinions, data, exhibits to be used by the expert at trial, her compensation, and the names of all other cases she has testified in as an expert in the past 4 years. (b) Discovery is limited to items that are relevant, and not privileged. • **Privileged Attorney Work Product** is the writings, notes, memoranda, reports on conversations with the client or witness, research, and confidential materials which an attorney has developed while representing a client, particularly anticipation of litigation. • The identity, knowledge and opinions of experts who are retained by counsel, but will not be used at trial is **not** privileged. (c) Courts may enter a protective order limiting discovery when needed to protect a person or party from "annoyance, embarrassment, oppression or undue burden or expense." (d) Discovery cannot commence until after the discovery conference. (e) A party who has made a disclosure under Rule 26(a) or who has responded to an interrogatory, request for production or request for admission must supplement or correct its disclosure or response in a timely manner if they learn that the disclosure or response is incomplete or incorrect or as ordered by the court. (f) Settlement conference must take place as soon as practicable to settlement is possible; if not a discovery plan is required. (g) Every disclosure requires a signature by at least one attorney and must state signer's address, e-mail address and telephone number.
30	Oral Depositions	Oral testimony of a witness taken and recorded under oath.
33	Interrogatories	Sworn written responses to a set of written questions given under oath.

Summaries of Selected FRCP Provisions, *continued*

Rule	Title	Description
34	Producing Documents, Electronically Stored Information, and Tangible Things, or Entering onto Land for Inspection	One party can demand the other produce documents and items or allow inspection of such items or land possessed or controlled by the other party.
35	Physical and Mental Exams	If the physical or mental condition of a party is relevant to the case and a showing of good cause is made, a court can order the party to submit to a physical or mental examination by a certified examiner. This is the only rule that requires court order.
36	Requests for Admission	A written request to admit, for purposes of the pending action, the truth of any matters including statements or opinions of fact, the application of law to the facts, and the genuineness of a document.
37	Failure to Make Disclosures or to Cooperate in Discovery; Sanctions	A motion for an order compelling discover can be used for failure to comply with discovery demands. Failure to comply with a discovery order can result in sanctions, including being held in contempt, except that the court will not hold a party in contempt for failing to submit to a physical or mental examination.
42	Consolidation; Separate Trials	(a) **Consolidate:** Allows court to consolidate existing actions pending, where the actions share common questions of law or fact. (b) **Separate Trials:** Allows court to sever claims when unmanageable or unduly complex, or when the presence of one claim threatens to prejudice another claim.
50	Judgments as a Matter of Law in a Jury Trial; Related Motion for a New Trial	**Judgment as a Matter of Law:** Judge grants a verdict without a jury under circumstances in which no rational jury could find for the party opposing the motion. **Judgment Notwithstanding the Verdict (JNOV):** Judge enters a judgment that deviates from the jury under circumstances in which the court determines the jury verdict is without merit. This motion must be made 10 days after jury verdict.
56	Summary Judgment	A motion for summary judgment resolves a case before trial. It gives court limited ability to look beyond the language in the pleadings to the actual facts that each side has marshaled to support its case. Court will grant summary judgment if there is *no genuine question of material fact* and the movant is entitled to judgment as a matter of law. Under such circumstances, the Court does not weigh evidence, nor does it determine credibility. The Court views evidence in a light most favorable to the nonmoving party to make a determination as to whether a party is entitled to a judgment as a matter of law.

Federal Jurisdiction

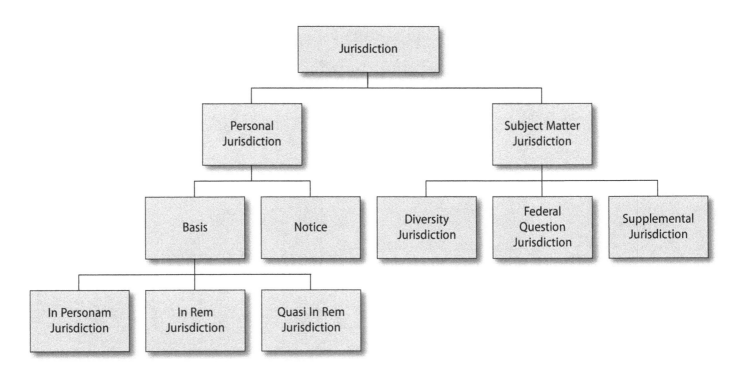

Personal Jurisdiction A court must have power over the defendant or the property that is the subject of the litigation. All defendants must have been properly served with notice of the litigation.

In Personam Jurisdiction A court's power over defendant's person (individual, company or other entity).

In Rem Jurisdiction A court's power over claims made about a piece of property or a particular status.

Quasi In Rem Jurisdiction Judicial attachment of a right or property owned by defendant within the forum state is used as a way of securing jurisdiction over the defendant. A *quasi in rem* action is commonly used when jurisdiction over the defendant is unobtainable due to absence from the jurisdiction. Any judgment will affect only property, as *in personam* is unobtainable. [A judgment based on *quasi in rem jurisdiction* affects rights to the property only between the persons involved and does not "bind the entire world" as does a judgment based on *in rem jurisdiction*.]

Subject Matter Jurisdiction Federal courts are limited to hearing cases based on questions of federal law that satisfy the requirements of diversity jurisdiction, supplemental jurisdiction, or have been properly removed from state to federal court.

Diversity Jurisdiction [USCA § 1332] Federal courts have jurisdiction over cases between citizens of different states and cases between citizens and foreigners, where the value or amount in controversy exceeds $75,000.

Federal Question Jurisdiction [USCA § 1331] Federal courts have jurisdiction over any claims arising under federal law so long as the federal question involved is integral to plaintiff's case and discernible in the complaint.

Supplemental Jurisdiction [USCA § 1367] Once a federal court has jurisdiction over a claim under § 1331 or § 1332, it may hear all claims that are related to the claims over which it has "original" jurisdiction, even where such related claim alone would not have qualified for federal subject matter jurisdiction.

Federal Subject Matter Jurisdiction

Federal Courts are courts of limited jurisdiction, meaning that they have authority to hear only certain types of cases. According to the United States Constitution Article III, federal courts have the power to hear the following cases because of their specific type of claim or controversy.

	Type of Jurisdiction	Rule	Definition	Amount in Controversy	Examples
FEDERAL QUESTION	Admiralty	28 U.S.C. §1331	Federal courts have jurisdiction over cases involving acts committed on the high seas and those involving contracts and transactions connected with shipping on the seas.	——	Federal court has jurisdiction over a property damage claim resulting from a boat collision off the coast of Florida.
	United States is a Party		Federal courts have jurisdiction to hear cases where the United States is a party.	——	Federal court has jurisdiction over a claim involving a bulletproof vest manufacturer suing the United States Armed Forces for breach of contract.
	Arising Under the Federal Constitution, Federal Law or a Treaty entered into by the U.S.		Federal courts have jurisdiction over cases in law and equity arising under the U.S. Constitution, federal laws and treaties.	——	Federal court has jurisdiction over a matter in which a tenant sues landlord for discrimination in violation of the federal Fair Housing Act.
DIVERSITY JURISDICTION		28 U.S.C. §1332	Federal courts have jurisdiction over cases between citizens of different states and cases between citizens and foreigners, where the sum of the value or amounts in controversy exceeds a certain amount, even where there is no issue of federal law.	More than $75,000	Diversity jurisdiction exists if a resident of Pennsylvania sues residents of Georgia and Florida claiming $76,000 in damages. There would be no diversity jurisdiction if either defendant were also a resident of Pennsylvania.
SUPPLEMENTAL JURISDICTION		28 U.S.C. §1367	Once a federal court has jurisdiction over a claim under §1331 or §1332, it may hear all claims that are related to the claims over which it has "original" jurisdiction.	——	The tenant who sues a landlord for discrimination in violation of the federal Fair Housing Act in the federal court can also attach additional claims arising under state law that are related to the claim, such as a breach of contract claim or a tort claim.
REMOVAL JURISDICTION		28 U.S.C. §1441	Defendant can usually "remove" a case filed in state court if plaintiff could have originally filed the suit in federal court, so long as defendant does so at the outset of the case. *Note:* Removal is not available in a diversity jurisdiction case in which plaintiff instituted the claim in the defendant's home state court.	——	A property damage claim as a result of a boat collision off the coast of Florida was brought in a Florida state court. Defendant can get the case removed to federal court since it could have originally been brought in federal court under federal question jurisdiction.

Minimum Contacts with Forum State for Personal Jurisdiction

A court has personal jurisdiction over an out-of-state defendant if defendant has the requisite minimum contacts with the state & exercising jurisdiction over the defendant is fair. In order to acquire personal jurisdiction over defendant, that individual must have purposefully availed themselves of the state's laws and the possibility of being haled into a court within the state must have been foreseeable.

		Case	Holding	Rule
MINIMUM CONTACTS		***International Shoe Co. v. Washington:*** International Shoe is a Delaware company based in Washington, and engaged in the manufacture and sale of shoes. International Shoe had salesmen on commission in Washington, but no offices there. The action, brought by the state of Washington sought to recover unpaid contributions to the Washington state unemployment compensation fund.	International Shoe's activities within Washington were systematic, continuous and resulted in a large volume of business. International Shoe also received the benefits and protections of the laws of Washington. Solicitation within a state by agents of a foreign corporation plus additional activities, render a foreign corporation amenable to suit within the forum state, to enforce an obligation arising out of its activities within the state.	A corporation that is protected by the laws of a state shall be subject to personal jurisdiction in that state. For a state to exercise in personam jurisdiction over a non-resident defendant, there must be minimum contacts between defendant, the forum and the claim.
CONTACTS RELATED TO THE CONTROVERSY	**Single or Isolated Activities**	***McGee v. International Life Insurance Co.:*** McGee, a California resident, is the beneficiary of a life insurance policy which International Life, a Texas company, refused to pay. International Life had inherited the McGee policy by acquisition of another company, and had no other contacts with California, other than McGee's policy.	California did not violate due process by entering a judgment against a Texas company engaged in a dispute over a policy it maintained with a California resident, even though this single policy which the company became responsible for by its acquisition of another company, was its only contact with California.	A single instance can be sufficient to establish personal jurisdiction.
	Sufficient Related Contacts Found	***Burger King Corp. v. Rudzewicz:*** Rudzewicz, a Michigan resident, acquired a Burger King franchise in Florida. Burger King sued Rudzewicz in Florida for breach of contract for failure to pay franchise fees. Rudzewicz objected to the Florida court exercising personal jurisdiction over him because he had never been present in Florida.	Although Rudzewicz was never physically present in Florida, his activities were directly targeting Florida and its residents, thereby subjecting himself to personal jurisdiction in Florida.	Where a forum state seeks to assert specific jurisdiction over a non-resident, the fair warning requirement is satisfied if defendant has purposefully directed activities at residents of the forum state and litigation results from alleged injuries that arose out of, or relate to those activities.
	Insufficient Related Contacts Found	***World-Wide Volkswagen v. Woodson:*** Woodson purchased a car in New York and was then involved in a car accident in Oklahoma. He started a product liability suit against the manufacturer Volkswagen in Oklahoma for injuries suffered.	Volkswagen did not sell cars, advertise, or maintain offices in Oklahoma, therefore Oklahoma courts were without the sufficient minimum contacts necessary to assert personal jurisdiction.	The foreseeability inquiry asks *not* whether it is foreseeable that a product might end up in a particular state, but rather, whether a defendant can foresee being haled into court there because she purposefully availed herself of that state's benefits.

Minimum Contacts with Forum State for Personal Jurisdiction, *continued*

	Case	Holding	Rule
CONTACTS UNRELATED TO THE CONTROVERSY	*Helicopteros Nacionales de Colombia, S.A. v. Hall:* Helicopteros, a Colombia corporation, purchased helicopters and trained some of its pilots in Texas. Subsequently, one of the helicopters crashed in Peru, and plaintiff filed suit against the company in Texas.	The fact that Helicopteros made purchases in the forum states was not sufficient to justify personal jurisdiction.	For a court to exercise *in personam jurisdiction*, a defendant must engage in systematic and continuous contacts with the forum state. For a single contact to form the basis of *in personam jurisdiction*, that contact would need be the subject of the litigation.
COMBINING RELATED AND UNRELATED FORUM CONTACTS	*Keeton v. Hustler Magazine:* Keeton, a New York resident, claims to have been libeled in five issues of a magazine. New Hampshire was the only state in which the statute of limitations for libel had not run. Hustler is an Ohio corporation with its principal place of business in California, and no other connection to New Hampshire, other than that it sells magazines there.	The court held that the aggregate of Hustler's contacts with New Hampshire was sufficient to establish jurisdiction.	An aggregate of related and unrelated contacts with the forum state are sufficient for personal jurisdiction.
NOTIONS OF FAIR PLAY AND SUBSTANTIAL JUSTICE	*Asahi Metal Industry Co. v. Superior Court:* A man injured in a car accident in California filed a product liability action to which Asahi Metal, a Japanese manufacturer who supplied parts to the car manufacturer, was joined.	The exertion of personal jurisdiction over Asahi was unreasonable and exceeded the limits of due process.	The substantial connection between defendant and the forum state necessary for a finding of minimum contacts requires demonstration that defendant purposefully directed its activities toward the state. The fact that a product made its way into the state, alone, is insufficient.

Venue Changes in the Federal Court System

Defendant can object to the location (venue) of the court where plaintiff filed a lawsuit and request that the case be moved to a new location. Such transfer requires that the case was originally eligible to be commenced in the alternate venue.

	Definition	Rule	
REMOVAL	Defendant can "remove" a case filed in state court if plaintiff could have originally filed suit in federal court, and the state court in which plaintiff commenced suit is not the defendant's home state in a case being removed to federal court on diversity grounds.	28 U.S.C. § 1441	State court → Federal Court.
TRANSFER	If a defendant moves for **forum non conveniens** on the grounds that there is a more convenient forum, the district court can "transfer" the case to another district court instead of dismissing it, so long as it could have originated there to begin with.	28 U.S.C. § 1404(a)	Federal District Court → Different Federal District Court.

Starting an Action

When a person or entity wishes to file suit against another person or entity,
the following steps must be taken to commence a lawsuit.

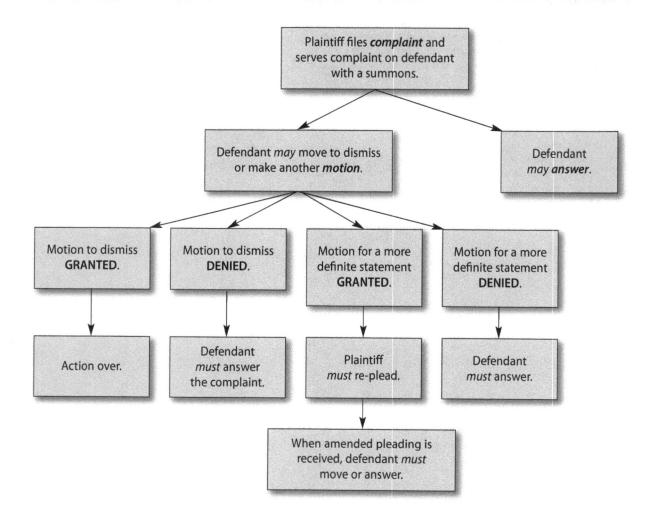

Plaintiff files **complaint** and serves complaint on defendant with a summons.

Defendant *may* move to dismiss or make another **motion**.

Defendant *may* **answer**.

Motion to dismiss **GRANTED.**

Motion to dismiss **DENIED.**

Motion for a more definite statement **GRANTED.**

Motion for a more definite statement **DENIED.**

Action over.

Defendant *must* answer the complaint.

Plaintiff *must* re-plead.

Defendant *must* answer.

When amended pleading is received, defendant *must* move or answer.

Pleadings

There are three primary forms of pleadings: (1) the complaint, (2) the answer, and (3) the reply.

DEFENDANT

1 COMPLAINT

Generally must be served within **120 days** of filing the complaint.

A first pleading in a lawsuit filed by plaintiff against defendant. It includes a statement setting forth the court's jurisdiction over the case, separately numbered causes of action that contain separately numbered paragraphs alleging facts on which the claims are based, and a demand for judgment in plaintiff's favor, for whatever relief plaintiff seeks.

2 ANSWER

Generally must be served within **20 days** of service of the complaint.

Defendant's response to plaintiff's complaint is called an answer. Defendant admits or denies each allegation of the complaint and can state defenses to each claim and assert counterclaims against plaintiff.

3 REPLY

Must be served within **20 days** of service of the answer.

A reply is an answer to defendant's answer. Replies are required when the defendant's answer contains a counterclaim and are otherwise allowed if the plaintiff obtained the court's permission.

PLAINTIFF

Defendant's Response to Being Served

A plaintiff begins an action by filing a complaint in a court of appropriate jurisdiction, seeking judicial relief against a particular defendant, and having the complaint served on the defendant. Defendant files a response in the form of an answer or a pre-answer motion to dismiss.

		Definition	Rule	Time to Respond
ANSWER	**NO WAIVER OF SERVICE**	A lawsuit is initiated by service of a summons and complaint, and defendant's response to the complaint is called an answer. Defendants can waive formal service of process; a defendant who elects not to waive formal service under FRCP 4(d), has less time to serve an answer than if she had waived.	FRCP 12(a)(1)(A)	Within 21 days after being served with the summons and complaint.
	WAIVED SERVICE	A defendant who timely waives service of process under FRCP 4(d) has more time to serve an answer.	FRCP 12(a)(1)(A)	Within 60 days after request for waiver is sent.
MOTION	**MOTION TO STRIKE**	Either party can request a court eliminate all or a portion of the opposition's complaint, answer, or discovery demands if they are immaterial, impertinent, scandalous or redundant.	FRCP 12(f)	On motion prior to pleading or within 21 days after service of pleading.
	MOTION FOR MORE DEFINITE STATEMENT	A motion for a more definite statement is a means of obtaining a more detailed motion from the opposing party before preparing a response. This motion will only be granted where the pleading is so vague or ambiguous that it would be unreasonable to require a reply.	FRCP 12(e)	Unless expressly stated otherwise, an opposing party has 10 days after an order demanding a more definite statement to comply.
	DENIAL OF PRE-ANSWER MOTION	If the defendant brings a pre-answer Rule 12 motion attacking the validity of the complaint, but that is denied or postponed until trial, defendant will have time after the court's denial to respond.	FRCP 12(b)(6)	Unless expressly stated otherwise, a responsive pleading is to be served within 10 days of the denial or postponement of the motion.

Pre-Answer Motion Defenses

FRCP 12(b) lists seven defenses that can be raised by defendant to attack the validity of plaintiff's complaint. Certain defenses do not need to be raised in a defendant's answer and can be raised later by motion. Other defenses are required to raised in the initial responsive pleading.

Defense	Definition	Waivable	Rules	Timing
LACK OF SUBJECT MATTER JURISDICTION	Defendant may seek to dismiss the complaint if the court lacks the authority to hear cases of this particular type or cases relating to this specific subject matter.	✘	FRCP 12(b)(1), FRCP 12(h)(3)	May be raised at anytime, even on appeal.
LACK OF PERSONAL JURISDICTION	Defendant may seek to dismiss the complaint if the court does not have power over this particular defendant or property and therefore cannot bind defendant to an obligation or adjudicate any rights over the property.	✔	FRCP 12(b)(2), FRCP 12(h)(1)	Waived if not raised in first response (by motion or answer).
IMPROPER VENUE	Defendant can object to the location (venue) of the court where plaintiff filed the lawsuit, and ask that it be removed from one location to another.	✔	FRCP 12(b)(3), FRCP 12(h)(1)	Waived if not raised in first response (by motion or answer).
INSUFFICIENCY OF PROCESS	Plaintiff must properly serve defendant the following: (1) a summons (formal court notice of a suit and time for response), and (2) a copy of the complaint. Defendant can object if plaintiff served an improper summons or complaint.	✔	FRCP 12(b)(4), FRCP 12(h)(1)	Waived if not raised in first response (by motion or answer).
INSUFFICIENCY OF SERVICE OF PROCESS	Plaintiff must deliver to defendant the following within 120 days of filing the complaint: (1) a summons, and (2) a copy of the complaint. Defendant can object if plaintiff failed to properly and timely serve her the summons and complaint.	✔	FRCP 12(b)(5), FRCP 12(h)(1)	Waived if not raised in first response (by motion or answer).
FAILURE TO STATE A CLAIM UPON WHICH RELIEF CAN BE GRANTED	Defendant may seek to dismiss the complaint if based on the facts alleged in the complaint, there is no legal theory under which plaintiff can obtain relief.	✘	FRCP 12(b)(6), FRCP 12(h)(2)	May be raised anytime before trial or at trial.
FAILURE TO JOIN AN INDISPENSABLE PARTY	Defendant may seek to dismiss the complaint if plaintiff failed to include certain parties who are indispensable to the case because of their relationship to the action.	✘	FRCP 12(b)(7), FRCP 12(h)(2)	May be raised anytime before trial or at trial.

The Answer

Defendant's response to a plaintiff's complaint is called an answer. Defendant admits or denies each allegation of the complaint, can state defenses to each claim and assert counterclaims.

		Definition	Rule	Examples	
	DENIALS	In her answer, defendant can deny the truth of any or all of plaintiff's allegations. Failure to deny an allegation in a required responsive pleading, other than an allegation of the amount of damages, is deemed an admission.	FRCP 8(d)	*General denial.* *Specific denial.* *Qualified denial.*	*Denial of knowledge or information sufficient to form a belief.* *Denial based on information and belief.*
	AFFIRMATIVE DEFENSES	An affirmative defense is asserted by showing that there are facts legally sufficient to excuse or mitigate defendant's liability. In most courts, defendant must raise all affirmative defenses when first responding to the claim, and a failure to do so may preclude assertion of that defense later in the case.	FRCP 8(c)	*Duress.* *Illegality.* *Fraud.* *Waiver.* *Estoppel.*	*Res Judicata.* *Contributory negligence.* *Statute of Limitations.* *Statute of Frauds.*
COUNTERCLAIM	**COMPULSORY COUNTERCLAIM**	In an answer, defendant must bring against plaintiff, any claim arising out of the transactions and occurrences that are the subject matter of the complaint. Defendant is required to plead a compulsory counterclaim and failure to do so is a waiver of the right to assert that counterclaim now and in the future.	FRCP 13(a)	*Carly and Chase get into a car accident and Carly sues Chase for personal injuries and property damage to her car. Any claim that Chase might have against Carly for personal injuries or damages to his car caused by the accident would be a compulsory counterclaim since it arose out of the car accident that gave rise to Carly's claims.*	
	PERMISSIVE COUNTERCLAIM	In an answer, defendant may bring any claim against plaintiff, even if not arising out of the transactions and occurrences that are the subject matter of the complaint. Defendant has the option of pleading a permissive counterclaim.	FRCP 13(b)	*Carly and Chase get into a car accident. A week later, Carly goes to Chase's home and punches him out of anger over the accident. Carly files suit against Chase for personal injuries and property damage to her car as a result of the car accident.* *Any claim Chase has against Carly for assault and battery would be a permissive counterclaim since it arose out of Carly's attack on Chase, which was a separate event that occurred at a different time and place than the car accident.*	

Types of Denials in an Answer

Defendant's response to plaintiff's complaint is called an answer. In her answer, defendant can deny the truth of any or all of plaintiff's allegations. Failure to deny an allegation in a required responsive pleading, other than an allegation of the amount of damages, is deemed an admission.

Types	Definition	Rule
GENERAL DENIAL	Defendant denies every allegation in the complaint.	**FRCP 8(b)(3)**
SPECIFIC DENIAL	Defendant denies the allegation in a particular paragraph of the complaint.	**FRCP 8(b)(3)**
QUALIFIED DENIAL	Defendant denies a particular portion of a particular paragraph of the complaint.	**FRCP 8(b)(4)**
DENIAL OF KNOWLEDGE OR INFORMATION	Defendant says she does not have enough knowledge or information to form a belief as to the truth of the allegation in a particular paragraph of the complaint.	**FRCP 8(b)(5)**
DENIAL BASED ON INFORMATION AND BELIEF	Defendant does not know the answer to a portion of the complaint with absolute certainty, but knows enough to form an answer based upon reasonable belief.	**FRCP 8(b)(5)**

Types of Affirmative Defenses in an Answer

Affirmative defenses claim that allegations complained of should be excused or mitigated. Each affirmative defense must be explicitly pleaded in the defendant's response; if a defense is not raised in the answer, it is waived. Below are some of the affirmative defenses listed in FRCP 8(c).

Defenses	Definition	The Defense Asserted
CONTRIBUTORY NEGLIGENCE	Plaintiff shares responsibility for the claimed injury.	*Jack serves a complaint against Jodi with a claim for damages resulting from their car accident that Jack claims was caused by Jodi speeding. In response, Jodi can assert that Jack contributed to the negligence in that had he not run the red light, they would not have crashed.*
DURESS	Force or threat of force, or other acts which had a powerful influence that precluded defendant from exercising free will.	*Pop Studios serves a photographer with a pleading alleging breach of contract. Photographer may assert that the contract is unenforceable because Pop Studios threatened to have the photographer harmed if she did not enter into the agreement.*
ILLEGALITY	Contract was illegal when entered into or became illegal because of a change in the law.	*Gun Manufacturer serves a complaint for breach of contract based on Retailer's refusal to continue sell its rifle. Retailer may assert the illegality defense if the law changed, making it illegal to sell rifles at Retailer's store.*
LACHES	A defense barring recovery because of undue delay in seeking relief, in which time it became unduly burdensome for defendant to be able to adequately defend the claim.	*Polly serves Duke with a pleading seeking to compel Duke to sell plaintiff property they had previously entered into a contract for five years earlier. In the interim, with Polly's knowledge, Duke had sold that property to a third party. In defense to the complaint, Duke may assert the laches defense based on the passage of time, and the fact that Duke no longer owns the property in question.*
RES JUDICATA	A final judgment was previously determined in an earlier proceeding on the same claim for which plaintiff is seeking relief.	*Mark sued Lauren for negligence arising from a slip and fall in her apartment; the court found Lauren was, in fact, **not** negligent. Two years later, Mark served Lauren again with a complaint, this time seeking recovery for emotional damages resulting from the same slip and fall. Lauren will successfully be able to raise the defense of res judicata because the claim for emotional damages is an attempt to relitigate a claim that was previously determined.*
STATUTE OF FRAUDS	The underlying contract is unenforceable because it is not in writing signed by the party to be charged.	*Walter serves Zeke with a pleading seeking recovery for breach of a land sales contract the parties had orally agreed to. Zeke may successfully raise the statute of frauds because land sales contracts need be in writing signed by the party to be charged.*
STATUTE OF LIMITATIONS	One of the claims may be true as against defendant, but the time in which to bring such a claim has expired.	*Luke serves Al with a pleading, which makes a malpractice claim against Al architect for damages as a result of defective design of his home. If Luke brings this claim 30 years after the house was built, Al can assert as a defense the statute of limitations, that the time within which to bring the claim has expired.*
WAIVER	One of the claims may be true as against defendant, but plaintiff explicitly waived her right to bring a claim.	*Sue serves Derek with a pleading, which makes a claim that Derek breached a warranty under their contract. Derek may assert that the contract contained a waiver clause in which Sue expressly agreed not to sue for breach of that warranty.*

Joinder of Parties

Procedure by which multiple parties with the same rights or against whom the same rights are claimed are joined as co-plaintiffs or co-defendants so as to consolidate potential claims and insure an equitable outcome for all.

Type of Joinder		Rule	Requirements for Claims	Jurisdiction Requirements
PERMISSIVE JOINDER		FRCP 20	Joinder of plaintiffs or defendants provided that the claims joined to bring multiple parties into the lawsuit: (1) arise from the same transaction or occurrence; AND (2) have at least one common question of law or fact.	Additional defendants to be joined must meet the requirements of personal AND subject matter jurisdiction since supplemental jurisdiction does not apply. In a diversity action, joinder of additional defendants must not destroy complete diversity among the parties. If no federal question exists, the jurisdictional amount must be met by each defendant individually.
COMPULSORY JOINDER	**COMPULSORY JOINDER**	FRCP 19	Compels joinder in certain circumstances where the adjudication of pending claims will be compromised without the involvement of the party sought to be joined. Defendant must be joined if service can validly be made upon her and defendant's presence would not destroy diversity.	Traditional diversity and amount in controversy rules apply.
	Persons Required if Joinder Is Feasible	FRCP 19(a)	Party is deemed necessary if: (1) in her absence, complete relief cannot be accorded among the existing parties; OR (2) the absent party's ability to protect her interest relating to the subject action may be impaired; OR (3) in her absence, the disposition of the action may subject the existing parties to a risk of double, multiple or inconsistent obligations by reason of her claimed interest.	Unless defendant's presence would destroy diversity, defendant MUST be joined if service can validly be made upon her.
	If a Required Party Cannot Be Joined	FRCP 19(b)	Where a required party cannot be joined, the court considers the following to determine whether the action may proceed: (1) the extent to which the absence of the party prejudices the existing parties; (2) the extent to which the prejudice can be lessened or prevented; (3) whether a judgment will be adequate if rendered in the party's absence; AND (4) whether the party will have an adequate remedy if the action is dismissed for non-joinder.	

Impleader, Interpleader and Intervention
Procedural devices to add additional parties to a lawsuit.

		Rule	Definition	Requirements	Jurisdiction Requirements
IMPLEADER		FRCP 14	Defendant may join a non-party who may be responsible for indemnifying or sharing in defendant's legal liability to plaintiff.	A defendant who believes that a non-party is liable for all or part of plaintiff's claim may implead the non-party for all or part of plaintiff's claims against her.	Diversity not required; third party claims fall within the court's supplemental jurisdiction. Venue need not be proper for third party defendant.
INTERPLEADER	**STATUTORY INTERPLEADER**	28 U.S.C. §1335	A person in possession of property (stakeholder), the ownership of which is or may be claimed by more than one party, can join those parties in a single action in order to determine the rights of the property.	(1) The claims of many people to a single piece of property or sum of money are in question; (2) Applicant makes a timely application to be heard as soon as it has reason to know that its interest may be adversely affected by the outcome of the pending litigation; AND (3) Applicant serves its motion to intervene on the parties to the case and explains its reasons for intervening in the motion papers.	Minimum diversity—only 2 adverse claimants need be citizens of different states, AND Money or property that is the subject of the suit must be more than $500.
	RULE INTERPLEADER	FRCP 22			Personal jurisdiction over all claimants. Where subject matter jurisdiction for the action is based on diversity, there must be complete diversity—all claimants must be citizens of states other than the one in which the stakeholder is a citizen. AND Money or property that is the subject of a suit must be more than $75,000.
INTERVENTION	**INTERVENTION OF RIGHT**	FRCP 24(a)	A non-party (the intervener) can bring herself into the case if she has an unconditional right granted by federal statute or is allowed by a court to join an ongoing litigation as a matter of right, without the permission of the original litigants.	Intervener has the right to intervene under a federal statute OR: (1) Intervener has an interest related to the property or transaction which is the subject of the pending action; (2) The lawsuit has a possibility of significant detriment to the intervener; AND (3) Intervener's interest is not adequately represented by the current parties to the case.	Independent subject matter jurisdictional grounds are required for intervention of right in a diversity case because such intervention does not fall within the court's supplemental jurisdiction.
	PERMISSIVE INTERVENTION	FRCP 24(b)	A non-party (intervener) may bring herself into the case if she has a conditional right granted by federal statute to join an ongoing litigation or is allowed at the discretion of the court.	(1) A federal statute confers a conditional right to intervene; OR (2) Intervener claim or defense shares a common question of law or fact with the pending action.	A permissive intervener in a diversity case must independently meet federal subject matter jurisdictional requirements. (There must be diversity between the intervener and the opposing side.)

Interpleader

An equitable proceeding brought by a stakeholder to have a court determine the ownership rights of rival claimants to the same money or property.

Type	Rule	Diversity	Amount in Controversy	Service of Process	Venue	Deposit/Bond Necessary?	
STATUTORY INTERPLEADER	28 U.S.C. § 1335	**Minimum Diversity**: At least two claimants must be from different states. The citizenship of the stakeholder is immaterial.	More than **$500**.	**Nationwide Service**: Process may be served on any claimant, no matter where in the United States that claimant resides or is found.	Anywhere that a claimant resides.	✔	The stakeholder must deposit the stake or post a bond in an amount equivalent to its value.
RULE INTERPLEADER	FRCP 22	**Complete Diversity**: The claimants must be citizens of states other than the one in which the stakeholder is a citizen.	More than **$75,000**.	Service within the state where the federal court is located or pursuant to the long-arm of the state.	The action can be tried where any of the claimants reside, where the dispute arose, where the property is located or where any claimant is found if no other basis.	✘	The stakeholder is not obligated to deposit the stake with the court or post a bond.

Crossclaims and Counterclaims

Procedures by which a party adds additional parties to a lawsuit as co-plaintiffs/co-defendants or an adverse third party, Crossclaims and Counterclaims are intended to make the legal process more efficient by avoiding courts having to consider the same facts multiple times.

		Definition	Rule	Asserted Against	Example
CROSSCLAIMS		A claim against a party on the same side of the lawsuit.	**FRCP 13(g)**	Co-party.	*Clothing manufacturer shipped 300 dresses to a buyer by truck. The dresses were damaged when they arrived and buyer refused to pay upon delivery. Manufacturer sued both buyer and the trucking company. Buyer did not know whether the manufacturer or the trucking company was responsible for the damage, so buyer served an answer containing a denial that she owed money to the manufacturer for the damaged dresses and a cross-claim demanding the trucking company compensate for damages to the dresses.*
COUNTERCLAIMS	**COMPULSORY COUNTERCLAIM**	Compulsory counterclaims are assertions that defendant makes against plaintiff, arising from the same transaction or occurrence that form the basis of plaintiff's complaint.	**FRCP 13(a)**	Opposing party.	*Josh and Masha are part of a two-car collision. Josh starts a personal injury lawsuit for damages resulting from that collision; Masha asserts in a compulsory counterclaim that Josh actually owes her damages for her injuries.*
	PERMISSIVE COUNTERCLAIM	Permissive counterclaims are assertions that defendant makes against plaintiff that arise from an event unrelated to the matter on which the plaintiff's complaint is based.	**FRCP 13(b)**	Opposing party.	*Adam sues Lindsay for defamation. Lindsay then asserts a permissive counterclaim for breach of contract alleging that Adam owes her money for goods and services provided.*

The Doctrines of *Res Judicata* and Collateral Estoppel

Once a final determination in a case is rendered, re-litigation of the same claim or issue is barred.

	Definition	Elements	Scope
COLLATERAL ESTOPPEL (Issue Preclusion)	A doctrine that prohibits the re-litigation of an issue of fact or law that has been determined as part of an earlier claim.	(1) There was a final judgment on the merits issued in the prior case, (2) The same issue was litigated and determined in the prior case, (3) The issue was essential to the judgment in the prior case, AND (4) The party against whom collateral estoppel is asserted had a full and fair opportunity to litigate the issue in a prior proceeding.	Collateral estoppel does NOT bar the subsequent litigation of issues that were not raised in the prior case, even if the issues could have been raised.
RES JUDICATA (Claim Preclusion)	A doctrine that prohibits raising, in a subsequent litigation, a claim that has been previously determined.	(1) There was a final judgment on the merits issued in the prior case, (2) Both cases involve claims about the same transaction or occurrence, that share a common nucleus of operative fact, AND (3) The parties in the subsequent case are the same parties, or are in privity with, the parties in the original case.	*Res judicata* bars re-litigation of claims that were previously litigated as well as claims that could have been litigated in an earlier case.

Methods of Discovery

Procedural devices used to obtain evidence and information possessed by the opposing party and relevant to the claim being litigated.

		Rule	Definition	Participant	Admissibility in Court
DEPOSITIONS	Oral Depositions	FRCP 30	Oral testimony of a witness taken and recorded under oath.	Testimony taken from opposing party, a witness, an expert intended to be called at trial by the opposition or any person thought to have discoverable material.	The statement will be admissible if the person being questioned is providing live testimony, AND The deposition statement: (1) can be used to impeach a witness,
	Depositions Upon Written Questions	FRCP 31	Oral responses to written questions taken and recorded under oath.	Testimony taken from opposing party, a witness, an expert intended to be called at trial by the opposition or any person thought to have discoverable material.	(2) is from an adverse party, (3) is from an adverse witness and used for substantive purposes if it conflicts with witness' trial testimony, OR (4) if the witness is unavailable to testify at trial.
INTERROGATORIES		FRCP 33(a)	Sworn written responses to a set of written questions.	Interrogatories may be given only to a party.	The answers of a party obtained by an interrogatory can be used for any purpose.
REQUESTS TO PRODUCE		FRCP 34	One party's demand that the other produce documents and items, or allow inspection of such items or land possessed or controlled by the opposing party.	Requests to produce are only appropriate to serve upon a party.	Documents and reports are admissible unless their contents are prejudicial, hearsay or otherwise determined to be inadmissible.
REQUESTS FOR EXAMINATION		FRCP 35	If the physical or mental condition of a party is relevant to the case, a court can order the party to submit to a physical or mental examination by a certified examiner.	Physical and mental examinations can only be requested of a party whose mental or physical condition is in controversy.	Requests for physical and mental examinations are almost always admissible in court.
REQUESTS FOR ADMISSION		FRCP 36	A written request to admit relevant facts not in controversy, eliminating the need to provide supporting evidence. The party from whom the admission is sought may admit, deny or object to each of the requested admissions.	A party may serve a request for admission on any other party.	Requests for admission conclusively establish the matter admitted.

Discovery

Disclosure of information essential for litigation. Generally, applies to any matter relevant to the pending action. Certain information is shielded from discovery for public policy reasons; such information is not deemed discoverable and does not require disclosure.

Material	Definition	Rule	Discoverable?
LIST OF DOCUMENTS INTENDED TO BE USED AT TRIAL	A copy or a description of all documents and tangible things in a party's possession that the party plans on using at trial.	FRCP 26(a)(1)	✔
INFORMATION ABOUT EXPERTS TO BE CALLED AT TRIAL	The identity of the expert and her qualifications, the expert's report, opinions, data, exhibits to be used by the expert at trial, her compensation, and the names of all other cases she has testified in as an expert in the past 4 years.	FRCP 26(a), (b)	✔
INSURANCE AGREEMENTS	The existence and contents of any insurance agreement under which the insurer will be liable to satisfy any judgment that may result.	FRCP 26(a)(1)(D)	✔
PRIVILEGED MATERIAL	Communications between attorney and client, spouses, doctor-patient, priest-penitent, etc.	FRCP 26(b)(5)	✘
PRIVILEGE LOG	A log that describes the nature of the documents, information or communications that will not be disclosed because of claims that such documents, information or communications are protected from discovery.	FRCP 26(b)(5)	✔
STATEMENTS BY WITNESSES	A person who makes a statement to a party (or her lawyer) may obtain a copy of that statement whether the person is a party or a non-party.	FRCP 26(b)(3)	✔
WITNESSES TO BE CALLED AT TRIAL	The identity and location of each person who the disclosing party plans to use at trial.	FRCP 26(a)(1)(A)	✔
WORK PRODUCT	Writings, notes, memoranda, reports on conversations with the client or witness, research, and confidential materials which an attorney has developed while representing a client, particularly in anticipation of litigation.	FRCP 26(b)(3)	✘

Discovery Limitations

Discovery is the disclosure of information essential for litigation. Generally, discovery applies to any matter relevant to the pending action. The following are certain categories of information that are shielded from the rules of discovery for public policy reasons and are deemed not discoverable and do not require disclosure.

	Definition	Rule	Elements
RELEVANCE	Discovery applies only to matters that are pertinent to the matter at hand. All other information is considered outside of the scope of discoverable materials.	FRCP 26(b)	(1) Any matter that is not privileged, AND (2) Which is relevant to the subject matter involved in the pending action.
ATTORNEY-CLIENT PRIVILEGE	Communications between attorney and client concerning the client's representation are protected from compelled disclosure.	FRCP 26(b)(5)	(1) Must involve communications (the underlying facts of the controversy are not privileged), (2) Between an attorney and a client, AND (3) The privilege must be claimed and not been waived by disclosure of the contents of the communications to persons outside the attorney-client relationship.
WORK PRODUCT	The writings, notes, memoranda, reports on conversations with the client or witness, research, and confidential materials which an attorney has developed while representing a client, particularly in anticipation of litigation.	FRCP 26(b)(3)	(1) Confidential materials (the underlying facts of the controversy are not privileged ONLY the communication about those facts), (2) Prepared by an attorney, AND (3) In anticipation of litigation.
OTHER PRIVILEGED COMMUNICATIONS	Based upon the status and relationship of certain parties, such as spouses, doctor-patient or priest-penitent, and to encourage open communication between them, their communications are protected from exposure during discovery.	FRCP 26(b)(5), FRE 501	(1) Was made with an expectation of confidentiality, (2) Is essential to a relationship or purpose protected by public policy, AND (3) The privilege must be claimed and not been waived by disclosure of the contents of the communications to persons outside the relationship.

Terminating a Case

The following are a list of procedural devices that may be used to terminate a case.

	Definition	Rule	Timing
PRE-ANSWER MOTION	Defenses may be raised by defendant to attack the validity of plaintiff's complaint. Where successful, the pre-answer motion to dismiss terminates the litigation.	**FRCP 12(b)**	The pre-answer motion to dismiss can only be brought prior to serving an answer.
VOLUNTARY DISMISSAL (NONSUIT)	Plaintiff may voluntarily dismiss the complaint once as a matter of right without prejudice.	**FRCP 41(a)**	Voluntary dismissal must be before an answer or motion for summary judgment is served upon plaintiff.
INVOLUNTARY DISMISSAL	Plaintiff's claim may be involuntarily dismissed by a court order when plaintiff fails to prosecute the claims or to obey court rules or orders.	**FRCP 41(b)**	Anytime.
DEFAULT JUDGMENT	If defendant fails to respond to a pleading, defendant is in default and subject to entry of a default judgment.	**FRCP 55**	After defendant's failure to timely respond to complaint.
MOTION FOR JUDGMENT ON THE PLEADINGS	A party's request to the court to rule in her favor based on the pleadings on file, without accepting evidence, as when the outcome of the case rests on the court's interpretation of the law. If evidence is accepted, it is treated as a motion for summary judgment.	**FRCP 12(c)**	After service of all the pleadings in the case but prior to trial.
MOTION FOR JUDGMENT AS A MATTER OF LAW	If there is insufficient evidence to support a jury's verdict, the court may render a verdict. **Directed Verdict:** Procedure by which the court removes the case from consideration by the jury and renders a verdict on its own. **Judgment Notwithstanding the Verdict:** Judgment rendered by a court in favor of one party, even though the jury found for the other party.	**FRCP 50(a)**	**Directed Verdict:** made after both sides have made their cases, but before the jury deliberates. **Judgment Notwithstanding the Verdict (JNOV):** within 10 days after judgment is entered.
SUMMARY JUDGMENT	Court determines there is no triable issue of fact for a jury, and that a decision can be rendered as a matter of law.	**FRCP 56**	Plaintiff may make motion anytime up until 30 days after discovery is complete.

Adjudication without Trial
The following are ways to terminate a case without going to trial.

	Definition	Rule
VOLUNTARY DISMISSAL	Plaintiff may voluntarily dismiss the complaint once without prejudice (plaintiff can bring suit again) by filing a notice of dismissal before an answer or motion for summary judgment is served upon plaintiff.	**FRCP 41(a)(1)**
INVOLUNTARY DISMISSAL	Plaintiff's claim may be involuntarily dismissed by a court order when plaintiff fails to prosecute the claims or to obey court rules or orders.	**FRCP 41(b), FRCP 19**
DEFAULT JUDGMENT	If defendant fails to timely respond to a properly served summons and complaint, defendant is in default and subject to the possible entry of a default judgment.	**FRCP 55**
SUMMARY JUDGMENT	Where there is no dispute as to the material facts of the case, and a party is entitled to judgment as a matter of law.	**FRCP 56**
MOTION TO DISMISS	A complaint will be dismissed for failure to state a cause of action upon which relief can be granted if the facts as stated in the complaint fail to articulate a meritorious claim from which plaintiff can obtain relief.	**FRCP 12(b)(6)**

Class Action Prerequisites

A class action is a lawsuit that allows a large number of people with a common interest in a matter to sue or be sued as a group. All four prerequisites MUST be met before a class action lawsuit can be brought.

	Definition	Rule
CLASS SIZE	The class is so numerous that joinder of all members is impracticable. Fewer class members are needed to satisfy the size requirement when the class members are more geographically disbursed.	**FRCP 23(a)(1)**
COMMONALITY	There must be questions of law or fact common to the class.	**FRCP 23(a)(2)**
TYPICALITY	The claims or defenses of the representatives must be typical of those of the class.	**FRCP 23(a)(3)**
FAIR REPRESENTATION	The representatives must show that they will fairly and adequately protect the interests of the class and provide competent legal counsel to fight the suit.	**FRCP 23(a)(4)**

Types of Class Actions

A single person or small group of people may represent a larger group or "class" of people who share a common interest so long as their action fits into one of the below categories.

Categories	Purpose	Requirements	Notice	Options for Opting Out	Relief	Example
FRCP 23(b)(1) ACTION	Where prosecution of separate lawsuits by individual members of the class would create a risk of inconsistent or varying adjudications.	(1) There must be a risk of inconsistent decisions, OR (2) There must be a risk of impairment of the interests of other class members who would not have been part of the individual case.	Court *may* direct appropriate notice to the class. Notice can be individual (*i.e. mail*) or mass notice (*i.e. newspaper ad*).	Class members may NOT opt out and are bound by the holding.	Monetary Damages.	*Recovery is sought from a limited fund.*
FRCP 23(b)(2) ACTION	Where a defendant has taken action, or refused to take action, with respect to a group of individuals, and final relief of an injunctive nature or settling the dispute with respect to the class as a whole is appropriate.	Suit must be for an injunction or declaration that would affect all class members.	Court *may* direct appropriate notice to the class. Notice can be individual (*i.e. mail*) or mass notice (*i.e. newspaper ad*).	Class members may NOT opt out.	Injunctive or Declaratory Relief.	*Imposition of a regulatory scheme that affects all members of the class.*
FRCP 23(b)(3) ACTION	Where questions of law or fact common to the members of the class predominate over any questions affecting only individual members, and a class action would achieve economies of time, effort and expense.	(1) Class action must be superior to other available methods, AND (2) There must be questions of law or fact common to the class members.	Notice to all class members at plaintiff's expense. Best notice practicable under the circumstances must be given to all class members. Notice must inform members that they *may* opt out.	Class members MAY opt out.	Monetary Damages.	*Claims for money damages.*

Contracts

Uniform Commercial Code

In every state except Louisiana, sales of goods are governed by statute, Article 2 of the Uniform Commercial Code (UCC).

Summaries of Selected UCC Article 2 Provisions

Below are summaries of selected provisions of the Uniform Commercial Code, which are intended to be used as a quick reference. Look to the actual Code for a more in-depth description of the law.

Section	Title	Description
§ 2-102	Scope	This Article applies only to sales of goods, and explicitly excludes transactions creating security interests in goods.
§ 2-201	Statute of Frauds	A contract for the sale of goods for $500 or more must be in writing signed by the party to be charged unless the contract falls within one of the enumerated exceptions: **Merchant Memo Rule:** A written confirmation between merchants, sent within a reasonable time to an individual who has reason to know its contents, and there is no written objection to the confirmation within 10 days. [§ 2-201(2)] **Specially Manufactured Goods:** If the contract is for the manufacture of specialized goods for the buyer, which are not suitable for sale to others in the ordinary course of seller's business, and seller substantially starts to perform or makes commitments for the procurement of materials to manufacture the goods. [§ 2-201(3)(a)] **Admission:** The contract is admitted by the party against whom enforcement is sought in pleadings or testimony before the court. [§ 2-201(3)(b)] **Performance:** The buyer makes a payment for the goods, or receives and accepts all or part of the goods. [§ 2-201(3)(c)]
§ 2-202	Parol Evidence	Contractual terms which have been agreed upon by the parties may not be contradicted by evidence of any prior agreement or contemporaneous oral agreement, but may be explained or supplemented by course of performance, course of dealing or usage of trade, AND by evidence of consistent additional terms, unless the court finds the writing to have been intended to be a complete and exclusive statement of the agreement.[1]
§ 2-204	General Formation	Contracts for sale of goods are formed in any manner that demonstrates agreement, including offer and acceptance or conduct that recognizes the existence of a contract. Contracts for the sale of goods do not fail for indefiniteness where a term or terms are left open,[2] so long as the parties intend to make a contract and there is a reasonably certain basis for giving an appropriate remedy.
§ 2-205	Firm Offers	A written offer signed by a merchant to buy or sell goods that gives assurance that it will be held open and not revoked during the time stated, or if no time stated for a reasonable time, but in no event may such time period of irrevocability exceed three months.
§ 2-206	Offer and Acceptance	Unless otherwise unambiguously indicated by the language or circumstances, an offer to make a contract shall be construed as inviting acceptance in any reasonable manner. [§ 2-206(1)(a)] An offer to buy goods for prompt or current shipment shall be construed as inviting acceptance either by a prompt promise to ship or by the prompt or current shipment of conforming OR nonconforming goods; however, if seller ships non-conforming goods, she will not be considered to have simultaneously formed and breached a contract, so long as she seasonably notifies the buyer that the shipment is being offered as an accommodation. [§ 2-206(1)(b)] Starting performance is a reasonable mode of acceptance, however, if the offeror is not notified of the start of performance within a reasonable time, the offer may be treated as having lapsed before acceptance. [§ 2-206(2)]

---

1. Note: Courts have determined that evidence of fraud, mutual mistake, misrepresentation and condition precedents are admissible, and NOT barred by Parol Evidence.
2. Note: Failure to include a quantity term will cause a sale of goods contract to be void.

Summaries of Selected UCC Article 2 Provisions, *continued*

Section	Title	Description
§2-207	Acceptance with Additional Terms	A definite and seasonable expression of acceptance will be considered an acceptance, even if it contains additional or different terms from those in the offer, unless such acceptance is made conditional on the offeror expressly assenting to the additional or different terms within the acceptance. [§2-207(1)] If the parties are BOTH merchants, additional terms contained in the acceptance will become part of the contract unless: (1) the offer expressly limits acceptance to the terms of the offer, (2) the additional terms would materially change the contract, OR (3) the offeror notifies the offeree within a reasonable time that she objects to the additional terms. [§2-207(2)] Conduct of the parties which recognizes the existence of a contract is sufficient to establish a contract for sale of goods even if the writing alone between the parties would be insufficient to form a contract. [§2-207(3)]
§2-209	Modification, Rescission, Waiver	An agreement modifying a contract for sale of goods does not need consideration to be binding, provided the modification is in good faith. [§2-209(1)]³ If the original contract expressly prohibits modification or rescission without a signed writing, then modification or rescission must be in writing. [§2-209(2)] An oral modification of a contract for the sale of goods that is unenforceable because it needs to be in writing, can still operate effectively as a waiver of a condition within the original contract. [§2-209(4)] A party who has waived a portion of a contract not yet performed may retract the waiver so long as she reasonably notifies the other party that strict performance of the waived term is required, unless requiring such strict performance would be unjust because of a material change of position in reliance on the waiver. [§2-209(5)]
§2-210	Assignment of Rights and Delegation of Duties	Unless the contract expressly provides to the contrary, or an assignment would materially alter the parties' expectations under the contract, all rights or duties (obligations) of either buyer or seller can be assigned to a third party.⁴ The assignment of rights to a third party bars the original party entitled to said rights from enforcing those rights; nonetheless, the delegation of duties does not relieve the original obligor from liability for performance under the terms of the contract.
§2-302	Unconscionable Term or Contract	If a court finds a contract or any of its clauses to be unconscionable at the time it was made, the court may refuse to enforce it or enforce the remainder of the contract without the unconscionable clause or may limit the application of any unconscionable clause as to avoid an unconscionable result.⁵
§2-305	Open Price Term	A contract for the sale of goods in which a price term is missing or undetermined will not render the contract unenforceable, provided the parties intended to enter into a contract. The price will be a reasonable price at the time of delivery.
§2-306	Output, Requirements and Exclusive Dealings	A term which measures quantity by the output of the seller or the requirements of the buyer means such actual output or requirements as may occur in good faith. [§2-306(1)] Output or requirements terms are a substitute for the quantity term otherwise mandated to be in all contracts for sale of goods. A lawful agreement for exclusive dealing in goods imposes an obligation by seller to use best efforts to supply the goods and by buyer to use best efforts to promote their sale. [§2-306(2)]
§2-308	Absence of Specified Place for Delivery	If a contract does not specify where goods are to be delivered, the place for delivery is seller's place of business, or if seller does not have a place of business, her residence, unless the goods are specifically identified goods and known by the parties to be somewhere other than seller's place of business or residence, then that location is the place of delivery.

---

3. Note: The ability to modify a contract without additional consideration is a requirement separate and apart from the writing requirement under the Statute of Frauds; therefore even if a modification does not require additional consideration, it may still require a writing signed by the party if the modification falls within the Statute of Frauds.

4. Note: The right to collect money is always assignable, and cannot be limited by a term of contract barring the assignment of contractual rights or obligations.

5. Note: A contract or its terms is unconscionable when it is determined to be extremely unjust or overwhelmingly one sided in favor of the party in the superior bargaining position.

Summaries of Selected UCC Article 2 Provisions, *continued*

Section	Title	Description
§2-309	Absence of Specified Time of Delivery; Notice of Termination	If the contract is silent as to the time for shipment, delivery or performance, the time shall be within a reasonable time.
§2-310	Time for Payment	Absent a provision in the contract to the contrary, payment will be due at the time and place where the buyer is to receive the goods.
§2-312	Warranty of Title	All contracts for the sale of goods have a warranty that the seller has good title to the goods.
§2-313	Express Warranties	An affirmation of fact or promise in the contract that the goods being sold shall conform to the description.
§2-314	Implied Warranty; Merchantability; Usage of Trade	Absent a provision in the contract to the contrary, a merchant seller impliedly warrants in every contract for sale of goods that the goods sold are merchantable and therefore fit for the ordinary purpose for which such goods are used.
§2-315	Implied Warranty: Fitness for a Particular Purpose	Absent a provision in the contract to the contrary, any seller who i) has reason to know buyer intends to use the goods for a particular purpose, and ii) that buyer is relying on the seller's skill or judgment in the selection of suitable goods, impliedly warrants that the goods are fit for the particular purpose.
§2-316	Disclaimer of Warranties	A disclaimer of the warranty of merchantability i) must mention the word "merchantability," and ii) in a written contract, must be conspicuous. A disclaimer of the warranty of fitness for a particular purpose i) must be in writing, and ii) must be conspicuous.
§2-319	FOB Terms	The term FOB means "Free on Board." It controls which party to the contract bears the risk of loss while goods are in transit from seller to buyer. The term "FOB Buyer's Place of Business" places the risk of loss on the seller while the goods are in transit. The term "FOB Seller's Place of Business" places the risk of loss on the buyer while the goods are in transit.
§2-507	Time of Payment	Absent a provision in the contract to the contrary, tender of delivery entitles seller to payment for the goods.
§2-508	Cure by Seller of Improper Tender of Delivery; Replacement	Where seller tenders delivery of nonconforming goods prior to the time performance is due, seller may cure the non-conformity within the time remaining for performance upon reasonable notice to the buyer. [§2-508(1)] Seller has a limited right to cure non-conformity <u>after</u> the time for performance if she had reason to believe: i) the non-conforming goods would be acceptable to the buyer, OR ii) the buyer would be satisfied with the non-conforming goods and a money allowance. [§2-508(2)]
§2-509	Risk of Loss	Absent an FOB term or a provision in the contract to the contrary, i) Where the contract for sale of goods requires shipment to a particular destination, risk of loss remains with the seller until delivery to the destination, at which point risk of loss transfers to the buyer; ii) Where the contract for sale of goods does not identify a particular destination, risk of loss remains with the seller until delivery to a place where buyer is able to take delivery.
§2-510	Breach of Contract and Risk of Loss	Risk of loss remains with seller when the goods delivered fail to conform to the terms of the contract, and buyer rightfully rejects the goods.
§2-601	Buyer's Rights on Improper Delivery	Absent a provision in the contract to the contrary, if the goods or tender of delivery fail *in any respect* to conform to the contract, buyer may (1) reject the whole; OR (2) accept the whole; OR (3) accept some commercial unit or units and reject the rest.

Summaries of Selected UCC Article 2 Provisions, *continued*

Section	Title	Description
§2-602	Manner and Effect of Rightful Rejection	Rejection must occur within a reasonable time and upon reasonable notice to the seller after the goods are delivered.
§2-608	Revocation After Acceptance	Buyer may revoke acceptance within a reasonable time after acceptance, provided the defect or non-conformity could not reasonably have been discovered earlier. A buyer who so revokes has the same rights and duties with regard to the goods involved as if she had rejected them.
§2-609	Right to Adequate Assurances on Performance	When reasonable grounds for insecurity arise with respect to the performance of either party, the other may demand in writing adequate assurance of performance, and until such assurance is received may, if commercially reasonable, suspend any performance for which she has not already received the agreed return. [§2-609(1)] Failure to provide assurances within 30 days may be treated as a breach of contract.
§2-610	Anticipatory Repudiation	Where either party unequivocally indicates that they will not perform their obligation under the contract, the injured party may immediately treat the contract as breached, and i) await performance by the repudiating party for a commercially reasonable time, OR ii) resort to any remedy for breach, AND iii) in either case, suspend her own performance.
§2-611	Retraction of Anticipatory Repudiation	The unequivocal indication that a party will not perform may be retracted at any time without penalty provided the injured party has not cancelled, materially changed her position in reliance on the repudiation, or otherwise treated the repudiation as final.
§2-612	Breach of Installment Contract	Each installment of an installment contract is treated as its own separate contract, and thus a nonconforming installment is generally not regarded as a breach of the contract as a whole, and a buyer may reject an installment, which is non-conforming if the non-conformity substantially impairs the value of that installment and cannot be cured. [§2-612(2)] Nonetheless, buyer has the right to cancel the entire installment contract if the defective installment substantially impairs the value of the whole contract. [§2-612(3)]
§2-613	Casualty to Identified Goods	If a contract is for specifically identified goods which are damaged or destroyed through no fault of either party, prior to the risk of loss passing to the buyer, the contract is avoided, or buyer may accept the goods with an agreed to price allowance reflecting the loss in value.
§2-615	Excuse by Failure of Presupposed Conditions	Seller's non-delivery or delayed delivery is excused if performance has been made impracticable by the occurrence or non-occurrence of an event, which was a basic assumption of the contract. Seller must provide buyer with reasonable notice of the delay.
§2-702	Seller Remedies Upon Buyer Insolvency	Where seller discovers buyer is insolvent, she may refuse to deliver except for cash, and stop delivery of goods in transit. [§2-702(1)] Where seller discovers buyer has received goods on credit while insolvent, she may reclaim the goods upon demand made within ten days after receipt. [§2-702(2)] Seller who successfully exercises a right to reclaim goods has no further right to sue for breach of contract. [§2-702(3)]
§2-706	Resale of Good	A non-breaching seller may mitigate damages by reselling goods in a commercially reasonable manner by way of a public or private resale. In the case of a private resale, seller must provide buyer reasonable notice of the resale.
§2-708	Seller Damages for Non-Acceptance or Repudiation	The measure of damages from the non-accepting buyer is the difference between the market price and the contract price plus incidental damages less any expenses saved as a result of the breach. [§2-708(1)] If the measure of damages in §2-708(1) is inadequate to put the seller in as good a position as performance under the contract, then the measure of damages is the lost profit plus incidental damages. [§2-708(2)][6]

6. Note: Lost profits are the measure of damages usually used by a high volume retailer capable of selling as many items as the retailer has orders.

Summaries of Selected UCC Article 2 Provisions, *continued*

Section	Title	Description
§2-712	**Cover and Buyer Procurement of Substituted Goods**	Non-breaching buyers may purchase conforming goods from another source and recover from a breaching seller the difference between the contract price and the market price paid.
§2-713	**Buyer Damages for Non-Acceptance or Repudiation**	The measure of damages for seller's breach is the difference between the market price and the contract price, together with any incidental and consequential damages. [§2-713(1)]
§2-715	**Incidental and Consequential Damages**	**Incidental Damages:** Reasonable expenses incurred from a breach of contract, including but not limited to inspection, repair, transport, care, and storage. (Also see §2-710) **Consequential Damages:** Losses caused by breach of contract that the breaching party knew or should have known would result at the time the contract was entered into.
§2-716	**Buyer's Right to Specific Performance**	Specific performance is a remedy that is generally limited to circumstances in which the goods at issue are unique. [§2-716(1)]
§2-718	**Liquidated Damages**	Damages that are agreed to as a term of contract in the event of a breach. Liquidated damages are enforceable only under circumstances in which the amount of damages agreed to are reasonable, and a measure of damages could not otherwise be conveniently determined.

Types of Contracts

A contract is a voluntary agreement to do or not to do something that is mutually agreed upon by competent parties and supported by consideration.

Type	Definition	Formation	Acceptance	Examples
EXPRESS CONTRACT	Created by language, oral or written, demonstrating agreement.	Formed when there is a meeting of the minds between the parties.	Acceptance can be by words of agreement, oral or written, or performance.	*The entertainer entered into an express contract when the club owner offered her money to perform on Saturday night, and the entertainer agreed.*
IMPLIED IN FACT CONTRACT	The terms are implied circumstantially from the parties' conduct, assumed intentions or relationship.	Formed by non-verbal conduct, when one party accepts something of value knowing that the other party expects compensation.	Acceptance is inferred from the parties' acts, conduct, or words even if they are not explicitly words of agreement.	*Harry sits down in a barbershop and gets his hair cut—there is an implied contract that Harry will pay the barber in consideration for the barber having cut Harry's hair.*
BILATERAL CONTRACT	Each party makes a promise or set of promises to the other.	Formed upon the mutual exchange of promises.	Acceptance by promise.	*In a contract for the sale of a house, the buyer promises to pay $400,000 in consideration for the seller's promise to deliver title to the house.*
UNILATERAL CONTRACT	One party promises to do or refrain from doing something in return for the other party's performance.	Formed when one side makes a promise and the other side performs.	Acceptance by performance.	*Hallie states, "Painter, if you paint my house before Saturday, I will pay you $1,000 when you are finished." The Painter completes the painting of the house on Friday.*
QUASI-CONTRACT (IMPLIED IN LAW)	An equitable remedy compensating a party relying on a representation to her detriment, or from conferring on another an unjust enrichment without compensation when contract law would otherwise yield an unfair result.	No contract is formed.	No acceptance, but rather, an equitable remedy is imposed by law.	*Mower arrives at the wrong house to mow the lawn. Homeowner knows Mower is at the wrong house, but allows him to mow the lawn anyway. Under a theory of unjust enrichment, Mower will recover for his services in mowing the lawn.*

Common Contract Clauses

Clauses commonly found in contracts.

Clause	Definition	Examples
ARBITRATION CLAUSE	Language specifying that all disputes under the contract will be resolved by arbitration.	*If a dispute shall arise between the parties, it is agreed that it shall be referred to for arbitration in accordance with the rules of the American Arbitration Association.*
CHOICE OF LAW AND FORUM CLAUSE	Language specifying that disputes arising under the contract are to be interpreted under the laws of a particular state and/or any litigation will occur within a particular state's jurisdiction.	*This agreement shall be interpreted under the laws of the State of New York. Any litigation under this agreement shall be resolved in the trial courts of New York County, State of New York.*
INDEMNIFICATION CLAUSE	Language specifying that one party will reimburse the other if certain liabilities are incurred.	*Subcontractor agrees to indemnify and hold harmless contractor against loss or liability arising from work done on behalf of contractor in building the house.*
LIQUIDATED DAMAGES CLAUSE	Language specifying an amount of predetermined damages due in the event of a breach of contract. To be enforceable, actual damages must not otherwise be readily calculable, and the amount agreed to must be a reasonable estimate of damages.	*Tenants canceling their leases before the end of the contract term shall pay liquidated damages in the amount of $20.00 per day for the remainder of the term, but in no event shall the amount due exceed $1,000.*
MERGER CLAUSE	Language specifying that all promises and agreements are included in the written contract. Prevents contracting parties from subsequently claiming the contract does not reflect their entire understanding, or was modified by a prior or contemporaneous agreement.	*This Agreement contains the entire agreement of the parties and will supersede all prior negotiations, agreements and understandings. This Agreement may only be amended by a written document duly executed by all parties.*
NON-WAIVER CLAUSE	Language used to protect a party who excuses the other's non-compliance with contract terms, and to prevent the parties' course of conduct from resulting in the loss of enforceability of the contract or a contract term.	*The failure by one party to require performance of any provision shall not affect that party's right to require performance at any time thereafter, nor shall a waiver of any breach or default of this Contract constitute a waiver of any subsequent breach or default or a waiver of the provision itself.*
SEVERABILITY CLAUSE	Language specifying that the contract as a whole remains enforceable, even if a term or terms of the contract are subsequently held to be void or unenforceable.	*If any provision of this Contract is held unenforceable, then such provision will be modified to reflect the parties' intention and all other provisions shall remain in full force and effect.*
STATUTE OF LIMITATIONS CLAUSE	Language that alters enforceable statute of limitations relating to the subject matter of the contract.	*The parties agree that any action related to an alleged breach of this Agreement shall be commenced within one year of the date of the breach, regardless of when the breach is discovered. Any action not brought within the year shall be barred, without regard to other limitation periods set forth by law or statute.*
TIME OF PERFORMANCE CLAUSE	Language specifying "time is of the essence" ensures that the time for performing the contract is treated as a material term of contract.	*Time is of the essence for the completion of the nightclub. It is anticipated by the parties that all work will be completed within one month of the date of execution of this contract, and any delay in the completion shall constitute a material breach of this contract.*

Requisites of a Contract

In order for a contract to be formed, there must be offer, acceptance and consideration. There must be mutual assent, or a "meeting of the minds" between the parties. In order for the parties to reach a meeting of the minds, an Offeror must make an offer and the Offeree must accept it.

	Definition	Elements
OFFER	An expression of willingness to contract on a specific set of terms, with the intention that if the offer is accepted, the parties will be contractually bound by the proposed terms.	(1) Offeror must make a commitment or promise to offeree, (2) Terms must be specific and definite, (3) Must create a power of acceptance in the offeree, AND (4) Must be binding on offeror, if accepted.
ACCEPTANCE	An expression of agreement to the terms offered in the manner prescribed or authorized in the offer.	(1) Offeree agrees to terms of the offer, AND (2) Agreement is in a manner deemed acceptable for acceptance of the offer.
CONSIDERATION	A bargained-for exchange between the parties in which each party must receive something of value in return for incurring a detriment.	(1) There must be a sufficient bargained-for exchange between the parties, AND (2) That which is bargained-for must create both a benefit and detriment to each of the parties to the contract.

Invalid Types of Offers

Communications that do not manifest an intent to be contractually bound do not constitute offers.

	Definition	Exceptions
SOLICITATION OF BIDS	A solicitation for bids is a request for an offer and NOT an offer, and therefore cannot be accepted to form a contract. Instead, it merely serves as a basis for beginning negotiations.	Solicitation of bids may result in a claim for quasi-contractual relief under a theory of detrimental reliance where the bidder knows or has reason to know that the solicitor is relying on the bid in making his own offer.
OFFERS MADE IN JEST	A proposal obviously made in jest is NOT a valid offer. When an offer is a joke, a contract is not made even if the offer is accepted.	If the speaker intends to create in the listener the impression that the speaker is committing himself to a particular proposal, and a reasonable person would so believe, then an offer has been made irrespective of whether the speaker was making the offer in jest.
ADVERTISEMENTS	Most advertisements are NOT offers to sell. An advertisement is generally construed as an invitation to make an offer.	An advertisement can be construed as an offer under circumstances in which the power of acceptance is limited to the first person(s) that fulfills the act for which the incentive is offered.
AUCTIONS	Items being put up for sale at auction are generally not regarded as forming an offer, but rather are solicitations for an offer from the audience.	Items being put up for sale at auction can be construed as an offer if the auction is announced to be "without reserve," in which case a request for bids or the highest bid will be deemed an offer.

Irrevocable Offers

An offer to contract is generally revocable at the will of the Offeror making the offer, but the following are excepted from the general rule.

	Definition	Examples
OPTION CONTRACTS	An option contract is an offer to enter into a contract that will remain open and irrevocable for a set period of time. The promise to remain irrevocable for a stated period must be supported by consideration in order for the option contract to be an enforceable irrevocable offer.	*Pete offers to buy 300 clocks from Sue. The offer states that if Sue pays Pete $10, he will keep the offer open for two months. If Sue pays the $10 to Pete, he will be unable to revoke his offer until the two-month period has lapsed.*
FIRM OFFERS	An offer by a merchant to buy or sell goods is irrevocable if the offer: (1) is signed in writing, AND (2) explicitly states that the offer will be held open. Said offer is irrevocable for the time stated or three months, whichever time period is less.	*Glove manufacturer sends storeowner a signed offer to sell 300 pairs of gloves. The offer promises to remain open for 60 days. Storeowner provides no consideration in return for the promise to keep the offer open for the 60 days. Nonetheless, because glove manufacturer is a merchant and the writing is signed, the offer is irrevocable for 60 days.*
PART PERFORMANCE	If the offer is for a unilateral contract, and the offeree begins performance, the offer becomes temporarily irrevocable and cannot be revoked by the offeror unless performance is not completed within a reasonable time.	*Melanie emailed Dave and offered him $500 if he paints her house. After reading the email, Dave went to Melanie's house and had painted two sides when Melanie decided she would rather wait until winter to have the house painted. Because Dave had begun performing, Melanie is unable to revoke her offer of $500, and will have to pay Dave provided he finishes painting the house within a reasonable time.*
DETRIMENTAL RELIANCE	If the offeror should reasonably expect to induce substantial action or forbearance on the part of the offeree prior to acceptance, and the offeree makes costly preparations in anticipation of a contract before actually accepting the offer, the offer will become temporarily irrevocable.	*Contractor solicits bids from subcontractors to install a roof so as to be able to prepare her own bid to build a home. The contractor relies on the lowest subcontractor's bid. If contractor's bid is submitted for consideration prior to subcontractor revoking her bid, the contractor has substantially and justifiably relied on the subcontractor's bid. Thus, the subcontractor's bid became irrevocable until the general contractor had a reasonable opportunity to notify the subcontractor of the acceptance.*

Acceptance with New or Additional Terms

When terms of acceptance diverge from the language in the offer, either by the addition of new or conflicting terms, the following determine whether a contract exists and what its terms are.

	Definition	Rules	Valid Acceptance of Additional Terms?	Valid Acceptance of Differing Terms?
COMMON LAW	Response will only be considered an acceptance if it is the absolute and unequivocal acceptance of each and every term of the offer.	**Mirror Image Rule.**	✘ The introduction of additional terms will result in a rejection and counteroffer, not an acceptance.	✘ The introduction of different terms will result in a rejection and counteroffer, not an acceptance.
ARTICLE 2 OF THE UNIFORM COMMERCIAL CODE	Acceptance is effective, even with additional or differing terms, unless it is expressly made conditional upon assent to the additional or differing terms.	**Battle of the Forms.** [UCC § 2-207]	✔ Any expression of acceptance or written confirmation will act as an acceptance of the original terms even if there are additional terms.	✔ Any expression of acceptance or written confirmation will act as an acceptance of any non-conflicting terms of contract.

Methods for Accepting an Offer

Creation of a valid contract requires offer, acceptance and consideration. Acceptance can be accomplished by unequivocally accepting the terms of the offer.

Methods of Acceptance	Definition	Examples
PROMISE TO PERFORM	A promise to perform is a suitable way to accept an offer, unless the offer explicitly requires acceptance by performance.	*Becky offers Jon $10 if he will wash her car over the weekend. Jon tells Becky he will wash her car on Sunday. Jon's promise is a valid form of acceptance, even before he washes the car.*
START OF PERFORMANCE	In a **bilateral contract**, starting performance is considered acceptance if the offer is open as to the method of acceptance, thus, starting performance by one party to the contract binds all the parties to the contract to complete performance.	*Peter promises to pay Lindsay $1,000 in exchange for her promise to paint his house. On Monday, Lindsay begins painting Peter's house. The start of Lindsay's performance is a valid form of acceptance, and thus both parties are obligated to complete performance.*
COMPLETION OF PERFORMANCE	In a **unilateral contract**, starting performance is insufficient, only completion of performance will be considered acceptance. Offeror must give offeree reasonable time for completion, but offeree is not required to complete performance.	*Melissa sends Michael a letter offering him $4,000 if he restores her old car. Michael buys a new engine and begins working on the car. After six months pass, Michael grows tired of fixing the car. Although Michael has done work on the car, his acceptance is invalid because he did not finish restoring the car. Michael is neither obligated to complete performance, nor is Melissa obligated under the contract to pay Michael unless the car is restored.*
ACCEPTANCE BY MAIL	Unless the offer expressly states otherwise, an acceptance is effective upon dispatch.	*Perri mails Alana an offer to buy her artwork on Monday. Alana receives Perri's letter and mails back an acceptance on Wednesday. Alana's acceptance is valid and effective as of Wednesday, even if Perri doesn't receive the acceptance until Friday.*
ACCOMMODATION SHIPMENT SENT	If a seller tries to accommodate a buyer by shipping non-conforming goods because the goods contracted for are unavailable, seller is making a counter-offer, which buyer can accept or reject.	*Soup Company has offered to purchase 5,000 russet potatoes from farmer. Due to a drought that destroyed the russet potato crop, the farmer sent 5,000 red potatoes as an accommodation. Shipping the red potatoes does not constitute acceptance, instead it serves as a counteroffer. Acceptance will occur if the Soup Company decides to accept the red potatoes.*
ACCEPTANCE BY SILENCE	Silence does not constitute acceptance unless the parties expressly agree to silence being a valid form of acceptance; the parties' prior course of dealings can determine whether the offeree's silence is regarded as a form of acceptance.	*Every week for the past year, seller responds to purchase orders from buyer by shipping or informing buyer items requested are out of stock. Seller's silence when receiving a purchase order from buyer will be deemed a valid form of acceptance.*

When an Acceptance Becomes Effective

*In order for an acceptance to an offer to effectively form a contract,
the acceptance must occur while the offer remains open.*

	Rule	Examples
MAILBOX RULE	Absent a provision in the contract to the contrary, an acceptance is effective upon proper dispatch.	*Jillian sends Kim an offer to buy her couch for $150. Kim writes an acceptance letter and mails it on Tuesday. Kim's acceptance formed an enforceable contract as of Tuesday.*
ALTERNATE MANNER OF DISPATCH	Even if an unreasonable manner of dispatch is used for the transmittal of an acceptance, the acceptance will still be effective upon dispatch so long as it is received within the time in which a properly dispatched acceptance would have been received.	*On Monday, Tim emails Marc an offer and requests Marc fax or email him an acceptance by Friday. On Tuesday, Marc mails an acceptance letter by regular mail, received by Tim on Thursday. Since the acceptance was received before Friday, it became an effective contract as of the Tuesday when it was mailed. If the acceptance had been delivered on Saturday, it would not have become effective since it was received after Friday.*
MISADDRESSED ACCEPTANCE	If an acceptance is improperly addressed, the acceptance is effective provided it is received within the time in which a properly dispatched acceptance would have been received.	*Yara intends to accept Quinn's offer, but accidentally sends her acceptance to Quinn's brother. Upon receipt, Quinn's brother faxes the acceptance to Quinn. The acceptance will be deemed effective when it was mailed by Yara since Quinn received the fax on the same day Quinn would have received it had it been correctly addressed.*
ACCEPTANCE SENT BEFORE REJECTION	An acceptance is effective upon dispatch and a subsequent revocation is ineffective, regardless of whether the revocation is received before or after the acceptance.	*Adam sends Lindsay a letter accepting her offer to buy her bike for $100. The next day, Adam trips and breaks his leg. Since Adam will no longer have a use for Lindsay's bike, he sends her a letter revoking his acceptance. Adam will be bound by the terms of the deal since he accepted Lindsay's offer and agreed to pay her $100 on the day he mailed his acceptance, thereby creating an enforceable contract.*
ACCEPTANCE SENT AFTER REJECTION	An acceptance sent after rejection is not effective unless the acceptance is received prior to the rejection.	*On Monday morning Ken sends May a letter rejecting her offer; on Tuesday he changes his mind and sends an acceptance. If the acceptance is received on Wednesday and the rejection not until Thursday, the acceptance will control, and an enforceable contract will have been formed.*
ACCEPTANCE LOST IN TRANSMISSION	If an acceptance is properly dispatched, it is effective at the time of dispatch regardless of whether it is lost in transit or never received.	*Nancy mails an acceptance to Wes on Thursday, but Wes never receives it. The acceptance is effective as of Thursday.*
ACCEPTANCE OF OPTION CONTRACTS	An option contract is a promise to keep an offer open for a period of time. Unlike a contract, acceptance of an option contract is not effective upon dispatch, but only upon actual receipt.	*Wendy makes Rob a promise that her offer will remain open for 3 weeks in consideration for his paying $50. One week later, Rob mails Wendy $50 and an acceptance. The acceptance will become effective only when it is actually received by Wendy.*
OFFER REVOCATION	A revocation of an offer is not effective until receipt. Therefore, if an offeree dispatches an acceptance before receiving a revocation of the offer, the acceptance will be effective and a contract will have been created.	*Mike offers to sell Al his motorcycle for $900 on Monday. On Tuesday Mike has a change of heart and sends a revocation of his offer by regular mail. On Wednesday, Al sends Mike an acceptance. If Al receives the revocation of Mike's offer on Thursday, the contract is effective because Al accepted Mike's offer before the revocation was received.*

Exceptions to the Mailbox Rule

To form a valid contract, there must be offer, acceptance and consideration. The Mailbox Rule is the general rule used to determine when an offer has been accepted. It states that acceptance becomes effective upon proper dispatch. Exceptions to the rule exist.

Exceptions	Definition	Examples
UNILATERAL CONTRACTS	A unilateral contract is one in which a promise is exchanged for performance. Accordingly, it will not matter when acceptance of a unilateral contract is dispatched, because unilateral contracts are only created upon an offeree's performance.	*Susan sends Adam a letter stating she will pay Adam $500 if he takes care of her dog while she is on vacation. Even if Adam signs the letter and mails it the same day, the offer will not be accepted until Adam has finished caring for Susan's dog.*
OPTION CONTRACTS	An option contract is an offer to contract that will remain open for a period of time. Acceptance of an option contract is effective upon receipt rather than dispatch.	*Wendy offered Robert a 30-day option contract to keep an offer to sell him her home for $500,000 open in consideration for his payment of $500. On Monday, Robert sent Wendy $500 and an acceptance. On Tuesday, before receiving Robert's acceptance and consideration, Wendy decided she was no longer interested in selling her home and telephoned Robert to advise him she was revoking her offer. The revocation was effective because Wendy had not received Robert's acceptance of the option contract, and thus her offer had remained revocable.*
ALTERNATIVE MEANS OF ACCEPTANCE	If an offer expressly states means by which the offer will be deemed accepted, the means stated will be the only sufficient form of acceptance, regardless of when another form of acceptance is dispatched.	*Rachel sent Jimmy a letter offering him $50 a week if he mows her lawn on Sundays. The letter states, "This offer will be accepted only when your letter of acceptance is personally delivered to me." If Jimmy emails Rachel an acceptance letter, it will not matter when the email was sent because personal delivery is the only valid form of acceptance.*
REVOCATION	Revocation is not effective until it is received by offeree, regardless of when it was dispatched.	*On Monday, Harrah mails Bob an offer to sell her car for $800. On Tuesday, Harrah gets an offer from Jamie to buy her car for $950. Harrah immediately mails Bob a letter revoking her offer. Although Harrah's revocation letter was dispatched on Tuesday, it will not be effective until Bob receives it, and he may accept Harrah's original offer until he receives the revocation letter.*
UNREASONABLE MANNER OF DISPATCH	If offeree accepts an offer by an unreasonable method, the acceptance will not be effective upon dispatch, only on receipt.	*On Monday, Tim emails Marc an offer and requests that Marc email him an acceptance by Tuesday. On Tuesday, Marc mails Tim an acceptance by regular mail. Although Marc dispatched his acceptance letter on Tuesday, Tim's offer will not be considered accepted on Tuesday because the acceptance letter arrived a few days after a properly dispatched email would have arrived. The letter will be only deemed an acceptance when it is received.*
MISADDRESSING	If offeree sends an acceptance to the wrong place, the acceptance will only be effective if and when it is received, and not upon dispatch.	*Yara intends to accept Quinn's offer, but accidentally sends her acceptance letter to Quinn's brother's house. Upon receiving it, Quinn's brother hands it to Quinn. The acceptance letter will not become effective on the day Yara mailed it, but rather on the day Quinn receives the letter.*

Termination of the Power to Accept an Offer

To form a valid contract, there must be offer, acceptance and consideration. Termination of the power to accept an offer may be held by Offeror making the offer or the Offeree to whom the offer is being made, and can occur under the following circumstances.

Ways of Terminating	Definition	When Power to Accept Ends	Terminating Party
REVOCATION	Power to accept an offer is terminated upon revocation of that offer.	Offeree can no longer accept an offer once she has received revocation of the offer.	Offeror.
REJECTION	Power to accept an offer is terminated if the offeree unconditionally rejects the offer.	Offeree can no longer accept an offer once it has been rejected.	Offeree.
COUNTER-OFFER	Power to accept an offer is terminated if the offeree makes a counteroffer.	Offeree can no longer accept an offer once she has made a counteroffer.	Offeree.
TIME LAPSE	Power to accept an offer is terminated if the offeree has not accepted the offer by the end of the period set by offeror, or after a reasonable period of time.	Offeree can no longer accept after a set time period for acceptance has lapsed, or if no set time limit, the power of acceptance will terminate at the end of a reasonable time.	Offeree.
INCAPACITY	Power to accept an offer is terminated if either party lacks capacity to enter into a contract, even if the offeree did not know about the incapacity until after the offer was accepted.	Offeree can no longer accept an offer once there has been a demonstrated lack of capacity by either party.	Either party.
DEATH[7]	If either party dies before an offer is accepted, the power to accept is terminated even if the offeree did not know about the offeror's death until after the offer was accepted.	Offeree can no longer accept an offer once there has been the death of either party.	Either party.

7. Note: Subsequent death or incapacity of the offeror does not terminate an offeree's power to accept pursuant to an option contract.

The Consequence of Adding New Terms to an Acceptance

	Contracts Governed by the Common Law	Contracts Governed by the UCC	
		Both Parties Merchants	Non-Merchants
ADDITIONAL TERMS	Under common law, the terms of the offer and the terms of the acceptance must be identical for a contract to be formed. **Mirror Image Rule** applies and no contract is formed because the adding of additional terms to the acceptance made the acceptance no longer "mirror" the offer.	If both parties are merchants, additional terms in the acceptance will become part of the contract unless: (1) the offer expressly limits acceptance to the terms of the offer, (2) the additional terms would materially change the contract, OR (3) the offeror notifies the offeree within a reasonable time that she objects to the additional terms. [**UCC § 2-207(2)**]	Contract terms limited to those contained in the offer. Additional terms added to the acceptance do not become part of the contract, but rather, are treated as a counteroffer.
DIFFERENT TERMS	Under common law, the terms of the offer and the terms of the acceptance must be identical for a contract to be formed. **Mirror Image Rule** applies and no contract is formed because the adding of different terms to the acceptance made the acceptance no longer "mirror" the offer.	If both parties are merchants and terms in the acceptance conflict with terms in the offer, the majority of states apply the **Knock Out Rule**, and conflicting terms will "knock each other out" of the contract, and missing terms will be replaced by relevant UCC standardized terms or "gap fillers." A minority of states, including California, apply the same rules for different terms as for additional terms under [**UCC § 2-207(2)**].	Contract terms limited to those contained in the offer. Different terms offered in the acceptance do not become part of the contract.

Sufficiency of Consideration

A contract must have consideration (a bargained-for exchange in which each party incurs a legal detriment) in order to be enforceable.

	Definition	Sufficient Consideration?	Examples
PROMISES TO MAKE A GIFT	A promise to give another party a gift.	✘ It lacks the "bargain" element of consideration.	Father tells son he will give him $500 for his 19th birthday. On the son's birthday, son demands father pay him the $500. However, the promise was not supported by a bargained for exchange, and thus the promise is not an enforceable contract for lack of consideration.
ILLUSORY PROMISES	A statement that appears to assure a performance and form a contract but, when scrutinized, leaves to the promisor the choice of performance or non-performance.	✘ It is not supported by consideration since the promisor does not legally bind herself to act.	A promise made in an agreement between a burger restaurant and a beef sales person whereby the burger restaurant promised to purchase as much beef "as its owner might order," is illusory because it is giving the burger restaurant the option to buy no beef and therefore does not provide sufficient consideration.
ALEATORY PROMISES	A promise where one party conditions performance upon the occurrence of a future event not within her control.	✔ The happening of a future event, even if outside the control of the parties, constitutes sufficient consideration.	Siblings agree that if their father leaves either of them any property in his will, they will share the property equally.
ALTERNATIVE PROMISES	If a bargain gives a party a choice of alternative obligations, each alternative on its own must constitute sufficient consideration for the return promise.	Maybe — Alternative promises in a contract will only be enforceable if each promise is detrimental to constitute sufficient consideration.	Ali agrees to give Bill either a watch or $300 if Bill paints her house. This agreement is valid since both of Ali's promises serve as valid consideration.
IMPLIED PROMISES	Obligations conditioned on facts and circumstances that are not expressly stated, but the circumstances reasonably impose the condition from the facts. *Note:* every contract has an implied covenant of good faith and fair dealing.	✔ Implied promises between parties to each use best efforts in performance of obligations under a contract is adequate consideration to form a binding contract.	Blaine grants Daisy exclusive rights to sell Blaine's product; Daisy promises to pay Blaine half of any of the sales she makes of Blaine's products. Although there is no express obligation on the part of Daisy to actually sell any product, the contract is enforceable because there is an implied promise between the parties to each use best efforts to create and sell the product.
FALSE RECITALS OF CONSIDERATION	When a recital of consideration exists solely to create the appearance of a binding contract, a court may decide the consideration is a sham, and thus the contract unenforceable.	✘ Recital that consideration was exchanged without actual consideration having been exchanged is insufficient to form a contract.	Grandmother promised to pay grandson $3,000 for good and valuable consideration received. Absent any indication that grandson incurred a detriment in return for the right to collect $3,000 from grandmother, the contract is unenforceable.
NOMINAL CONSIDERATION	When consideration is so small that it can be considered nominal, even if it may look as if consideration has been paid.	✘ If nominal consideration is given solely to create a binding contract, there is no true "bargain" and thus, the contract is unenforceable.	An agreement was made to pay $10 in consideration for the sale of a new corvette. Because $10 is not a realistic purchase price for a corvette, the consideration was only nominal and therefore insufficient to create an enforceable contract.

Sufficiency of Consideration, *continued*

	Definition	Sufficient Consideration?	Examples
PAST CONSIDERATION	When a contractual promise is made in exchange for a detriment already suffered by the promisee.	✘	It lacks the "bargain" element of consideration, and thus does not form an enforceable contract.	*In May, Amy helped Jane pack for her trip. In June, Jane promised to pay Amy $50 for her help. There is no exchange of consideration, and thus, June does not need to pay Amy, because you cannot bargain for a benefit that was already conferred.*

Order of Performance Under a Contract

Where a contract is silent as to the order in which the performance is to occur,
the following rules can help establish a timeline for performance.

	Definition	Effect of Occurrence of Condition	Examples
CONDITION PRECEDENT	A condition (or performance) must occur before a party to a contract is obligated to perform.	The occurrence of the condition triggers the obligations under the contract to come due.	*Jess made an agreement to pay her broker $10,000 if her house is sold by April 1. No payment is due under the agreement unless the condition precedent that the house be sold by April 1 occurs.*
CONDITION CONCURRENT	Conditions or performances under a contract that must occur simultaneously.	Once a condition has occurred, performance of the other is due.	*Nicki enters into a contract with Brandon to sell him her apartment for $250,000. Nicki's deed to the apartment and Brandon's money will be exchanged in the same transaction.*
CONDITION SUBSEQUENT	A condition (or performance) under a contract terminates a right or obligation.	The duty or obligation to perform under the contract is excused.	*CJ enters into a contract to sell Brady his house at the end of the year for $300,000 unless the zoning in the neighborhood is changed. If prior to the year end, the district re-zones the neighborhood, Brady will no longer have a duty to pay CJ, and CJ will no longer be obligated to transfer the deed to his house.*

Statute of Frauds

Contracts that need to be in writing in order to be enforceable are within the Statute of Frauds. These specific types of contracts MUST be put in writing and signed by the party to be charged in order to be enforceable.

Categories	Rule	Examples of Contracts that MUST be in Writing	Notes
MARRIAGE CONTRACTS	A promise for which the consideration is marriage or a promise of marriage is unenforceable unless it is in writing and signed by the party to be charged.	*A contract in which a man promises to support a woman's child if they married.*	Agreements made in contemplation of marriage and requiring a writing signed by the party to be charged do not include mutual promises to marry.
CONTRACTS LASTING OVER ONE YEAR	If a promise contained in a contract cannot be completed within one year from its creation, it is unenforceable unless it is in writing signed by the party to be charged.	*Employment contract entered into on December 1, 2012, which requires employment from January 1, 2013 through December 31, 2013 must be in writing signed by the party to be charged in order to be enforceable.* *A contract promising employment for the rest of employee's life need not be in writing since it is possible the contract will be completed in less than a year.*	It is the date a contract is entered into rather than the dates on which performance is to occur which controls whether the Statute of Frauds applies. In order for the Statute of Frauds to control, the contract must be one which CANNOT be performed within a year, rather than one that is unlikely to be performed within a year.
LAND CONTRACTS	A promise to transfer an interest in land is unenforceable unless it is in writing signed by the party to be charged. An exception exists under circumstances in which a purchaser makes partial payment and makes improvements and/or takes possession of the land.	*A contract for the sale of 22 Elm Street.*	"Transfer" does _not_ include leasing the right to use land, therefore an oral lease for 3 months would not be subject to the writing requirement of the Statute of Frauds. Leasing land for more than one year would be a contract falling under the statute of frauds requiring contracts that cannot be performed within a year to be in writing signed by the party to be charged.
CONTRACTS FOR THE SALE OF GOODS	A contract for the sale of goods for a price of $500 or more is unenforceable unless it is in writing signed by the party to be charged. Excepted from this rule are sale of goods contracts evidenced by a merchant memo, and contracts for specially manufactured goods, admission and performance.	*A contract for the sale of $900 worth of artwork.*	A contract for sale of goods that was over $500, and subsequently was modified to less than $500, does not require the modification to be in writing signed by the party to be charged; however, an oral contract for the sale of goods for less than $500 that is subsequently modified to be more than $500 is governed by the Statute of Frauds, and requires the modification to be in a writing signed by the party to be charged.
SURETYSHIP CONTRACTS	A promise to pay for the debt of another is unenforceable unless it is in writing.	*An agreement through which a person assumes liability for another already bound, either in whole or in part, for their debt.*	A suretyship can also be a promise to answer for the duty of another.

Battle of the Forms [UCC § 2-207]

Creation of a valid contract requires offer, acceptance and consideration. Under the UCC, acceptance may be valid even if it states terms additional to or different from the offer. § 2-207 is used to determine: (1) whether a contract exists, and if so, (2) what the terms are. Whether terms become part of the contract depends on the parties' status.

Acceptance Terms	Both Parties Merchants	One Party NOT a Merchant
IDENTICAL TERMS	Offeree's response automatically operates as an acceptance if it has the same terms as the offer.	Offeree's response automatically operates as an acceptance if it has the same terms as the offer.
ADDITIONAL TERMS	Additional terms automatically become part of the contract unless: (1) The original offer expressly limits acceptance to the terms of the offer, OR (2) Additional terms would materially alter the contract, OR (3) Objection to the additional terms is given in a reasonable time.	An additional term does not automatically become part of the contract and can only become part of the contract if the offeror explicitly assents to it as if it were an independent offer.
DIFFERENT TERMS	Most jurisdictions apply the **Knock-Out Rule**, which states that conflicting clauses in an offer and an acceptance "knock each other out," so that neither clause enters the contract. Instead, a UCC gap-filler provision is used to replace the conflicting term. A minority of courts treat different terms like additional terms and will consider them to be part of the contract unless: (1) The offer expressly limits acceptance to the terms of the offer, OR (2) Different terms would materially alter the offer, OR (3) Objection to the different terms is given in a reasonable time.	Most jurisdictions apply the **Knock-Out Rule**, which states that conflicting clauses in an offer and an acceptance "knock each other out," so that neither clause enters the contract. Instead, a UCC gap-filler provision is used to replace the missing term.

UCC Gap Fillers

Gap fillers supply ambiguous or missing terms so as to prevent an otherwise valid contract from being rendered void. UCC mandates that every contract for sale of goods contain a quantity term, and thus, the absence of a quantity term renders the contract void.

Term	Issue	UCC Section	Gap Filler
PRICE TERM	The contract is silent as to price. The price was to be agreed upon by the parties, and there is no agreement. The price was to be determined by a third party, but could not be so determined.	§ 2-305(1)	The price will be a reasonable price at the time of delivery.
DELIVERY LOCATION	The contract does not specify where the goods are to be delivered.	§ 2-308	Delivery will be seller's place of business, or, if seller does not have a place of business, seller's residence; however, if the goods are known to be in a place other than seller's place of business or residence at the time of contract, said place will be the place of delivery.
TIME FOR SHIPMENT OR DELIVERY	The contract is silent as to the time for shipment or delivery.	§ 2-309	The time will be within a reasonable time.
TIME OR PLACE FOR PAYMENT	The contract fails to specify the time and place of payment.	§ 2-310	Payment will be due at the time and place where buyer receives the goods.

Unanticipated Change of Circumstances after Contract Formation as a Defense to the Contract

	Definition	Examples
IMPOSSIBILITY	Unanticipated events that are the fault of neither party and make performance objectively impossible, discharge the contract.	*A contract between Mr. Smith and the Magic Emporium states that Magic Emporium's magician, Magic Al, will perform at Mr. Smith's party. The night before the party, Magic Al has a massive heart attack. The contract specifies that only Magic Al is suitable to perform. Magic Al's unanticipated illness made the contract objectively impossible to perform, and thus, both parties are discharged from responsibility under the contract.*
IMPRACTICABILITY	If performance is possible, but infeasible or commercially unrealistic due to unanticipated circumstances, then the contract may be discharged.	*A tap shoe manufacturer enters into a contract with a dance clothing store to sell 5,000 pairs of steel toe tap shoes by year's end. Several weeks later, the country goes to war and the U.S. government passes a law requiring all steel made in the country to go to the manufacture of military weapons. Although the tap shoe manufacturer could import steel from a foreign country, the cost of an import license and the taxes would eliminate any possibility of profit from the shoes. The unanticipated steel shortage made the manufacture of the tap shoes infeasible, and the contract may be discharged as commercially impracticable.*
FRUSTRATION OF PURPOSE	If unanticipated events destroy the underlying purpose of the contract, the contract may be discharged.	*Painter and Homeowner enter into a contract for Painter to paint Homeowner's house. The night before painting was to begin, the house burned down through no fault of either party. The underlying purpose of the contract, to paint the house, is destroyed thereby causing the contract to be discharged for frustration of purpose.*

Third Party Beneficiaries

A person who is not a party to a contract, but who benefits from the terms of the contract. A third party beneficiary is either an intended beneficiary of the contract, or a mere incidental beneficiary who unintentionally benefits from the contract.

Type of Beneficiary		Definition	Beneficiary's Rights Under Contract	Examples
INTENDED BENEFICIARY	**CREDITOR BENEFICIARY**	A person who is not a party to a contract, but to whom the promisee of the contract has intentionally given the benefit of the promised performance under the contract, in order to extinguish or reduce a debt owed that person.	Once an intended beneficiary knows of and relies on the contract, her rights under the contract vest and she can: (1) Restrict or veto proposed amendments to or requests to rescind the contract made by the original contracting parties, AND	*Meryl agrees to sell her camera to Brian for $500. The contract states that payment should be given to Blake instead of to Meryl, to satisfy a debt previously owed by Meryl to Blake. Brian is the promisor, Meryl is the promisee and Blake is the creditor beneficiary since the contract was intended to directly benefit her.*
	DONEE BENEFICIARY	A person who is not a party to a contract, but to whom the promisee of the contract has intentionally gifted the benefit of the promised performance under a contract.	(2) Sue promisor for breach if the promisor does not perform under the contract. **NOTE**: creditor beneficiary may still sue promisee to recover the preexisting debt if she cannot recover against promisor.	*Howard takes out a life insurance policy. He agrees to make monthly payments to InsureLife in exchange for InsureLife's promise to issue a monetary payout to his wife Robin, when he dies. InsureLife is the promisor, Howard is the promisee and Robin is the donee beneficiary since she will receive the benefit of the contract when Howard dies.*
INCIDENTAL BENEFICIARY		A person who benefits from a contract, even though the original parties to the contract did not intend to benefit this person.	None.	*Erica owns a restaurant in a remote part of town. Taylor, who owns the property next to the restaurant, enters into a contract with a developer to build a movie theater on her property. If the theater is built, it will increase foot traffic in front of Erica's restaurant and raise Erica's property value. Although Erica is not a party to the contract between Taylor and the developer and neither Taylor nor the developer intended to benefit Erica, Erica will benefit from the contract. Erica is an incidental beneficiary of the contract.*

Void and Voidable Contracts

A contract supported by the mutual assent of competent parties and consideration is "enforceable." However, there are certain contracts that are unenforceable despite the presence of mutual assent and consideration.

	Definition	Examples
VOID CONTRACTS	A contract with no legal effect because it is illegitimate and unenforceable from the moment it is created. Contracts where a party lacks capacity or the subject matter is illegal are void.	*An agreement between a pimp and a prostitute would be void because prostitution is illegal, so it cannot form the basis of a legally binding contract.*
VOIDABLE CONTRACTS	A contract in which one party has the option of terminating the agreement because a valid defense exists to the formation of the contract. Common defenses which render a contract voidable include the failure to disclose a material fact, mutual mistake, fraud or misrepresentation, undue influence, duress or unconscionability.	*Jack was induced into signing a contract for a time-share vacation rental company by being mislead into believing that he could take his vacation anywhere in the world. In actuality, his choices were limited to vacation communities in the mid-Atlantic states. Jack can "avoid" the contract because there was either a failure to disclose a material fact, fraud or misrepresentation of facts that induced him to sign the contract.*

Latent Ambiguities in a Contract

Ambiguities exist when a contract term is susceptible to more than one reasonable interpretation, and the parties disagree on the meaning. Under such circumstances, terms will be interpreted against the drafting party.

Who Was Aware of the Ambiguity?	Rule	Examples	Was a Contract Formed?
BOTH PARTIES	If both parties were on notice of the ambiguity at the time the contract was made, there is no contract unless the parties come to agree upon the meaning of the ambiguous expression.	Bakery and Supermarket entered into a contract for Supermarket to buy 500 babkas a month for two years. Both parties were on notice that Bakery makes two kinds of babka, but it was not until after signing the contract that they learned that Supermarket understood it was buying only Bakery's chocolate babkas, while Bakery understood that it was selling both chocolate and cinnamon babkas. Since the parties did not intend the same type of babka at the time of contracting, no contract was formed and neither party is required to perform. This constitutes the defense of mutual mistake.	✘
ONLY ONE PARTY	If at the time of contracting, one party was on notice of the ambiguity in the contract and the other party was not, a contract will be enforced according to the interpretation of the party without notice.	Gus entered into a contract with Cup Manufacturer to purchase 600 shot glasses for his bar. After signing the contract for 600 shot glasses, it was determined that Cup Manufacturer intended to sell Gus 2 oz. shot glasses while Gus intended to buy 1 oz. shot glasses. At the time of contract, Gus did not know Cup Manufacturer made two different sized shot glasses, while this information was readily available to Cup Manufacturer. The contract will be enforceable as one for 600 1 oz. shot glasses because Cup Manufacturer was on notice of the ambiguity, and Gus was not.	✔
NEITHER PARTY	If neither party was on notice of the ambiguity at the time the contract was made, there is no contract unless the parties come to an agreement on the meaning of the ambiguous expression.	Buyer agrees to purchase cotton from Seller when it arrives on a blue ship. Later, the parties learn Seller has cotton being delivered on two blue ships, which are arriving with cotton deliveries in different months. Neither party was aware there were two blue ships. Accordingly, no contract was formed and neither party is required to perform.	✘

Judicial Interpretations of Ambiguities in a Contract

Ambiguities exist when a contract term is susceptible to more than one reasonable interpretation, and the parties disagree on the meaning. Under such circumstances, terms will be interpreted against the drafting party.

Rule	Definition	Rationale	Extrinsic Information Allowable?		Strictness
FOUR CORNERS RULE	Only the meaning of the text within the document is used to interpret the intention of the parties entering into the contract.	Where the parties have deliberately put their agreement into writing, it is presumed that the writing is intended to be the whole of the contract.	✘	Judge can decide whether a term is ambiguous only by looking within the "four corners" of the contract.	Most Strict.
PLAIN MEANING RULE	If there is no ambiguity on the face of the contract and no special meaning is attached to the contractual words by custom or usage, the terms are to be interpreted in accordance with their plain, ordinary and literal meaning. The clear meaning of the words must be applied.	The objective definition of the contract terms are controlling irrespective of whether the language comports with the intention of the parties.	✔	The plain meaning of the contract will be followed where the words used have a clear and unambiguous meaning, however, modern courts do allow extrinsic evidence to be presented to aid in interpreting the contract.	Moderate.
LIBERAL RULE	Evidence of the parties' statements during their pre-contract negotiations is admissible for the limited purpose of letting the judge determine whether the term is ambiguous.	If a term is ambiguous, look to the intent of the parties to determine its meaning.	✔	Extrinsic evidence can be used to determine whether a term is ambiguous.	Least Strict.

Types of Contractual Defenses

Once a contract has been formed, it can be determined to be unenforceable by reason of a defense. Defenses can be asserted based upon: (1) defects in the subject matter of the agreement, (2) the capacity of a party to contract, or (3) the failure of the agreement to qualify for judicial relief.

Type of Defense	Rule	Defenses	Rule	Examples
DEFENSES TO FORMATION	A contract will be unenforceable if the contract was not properly formed.	**No Mutual Assent**	A contract cannot validly be formed unless the parties reach a meeting of the minds about the terms. If the parties did not reach the "same bargain at the same time," there is no contract.	*Mutual Mistake.* *Misunderstanding.* *Misrepresentation.*
		No Consideration	A contract cannot validly be formed unless it contains a bargained-for exchange between the parties.	*A promise to make a gift.* *Preexisting duty.*
		Statute of Frauds	Certain types of contracts will not be enforced unless they are in writing signed by the party to be charged.	*An oral contract for the sale of land.* *Contracts that cannot be performed within a year.* *Sale of goods for $500 or more.*
LACK OF CAPACITY DEFENSES	Once a contract is formed, it is possible that it will be unenforceable due to a lack of consent or an inability to consent as a result of being a member of a protected class.	**Legal Incapacity**	A contract cannot validly be entered into by a person in a protected class, who the law deems incapable of understanding the consequences of incurring binding obligations.	*Infancy.* *Mental Incapacity.* *Intoxication.*
		Lack of Free Will	A contract will not be valid if one party used coercion, threats or acts to influence the other in a way that precluded the other party from exercising free will when contracting.	*Duress.* *Undue Influence.* *Fraud.*
DEFENSES TO ENFORCEMENT	Once a contract has been formed, it is possible that it will be unenforceable because enforcement of its terms would cause an unfair result.	**Changed Circumstances**	Required performance under a contract will be excused if circumstances change in a such a way that the parties did not know or have reason to know would occur, and such circumstances render performance extremely difficult or impossible.	*Impossibility.* *Impracticability.* *Frustration of purpose.*
		Unconscionability	A court may choose not to enforce a contract, which had an absence of meaningful choice for one party and unreasonably favorable terms for the other at the time of contract formation.	*Party in a superior bargaining position taking undue advantage of the lack of experience of the other.*
		Against Public Policy	A contract will not be enforced if it differs from the basic policies forming the foundation of public laws even though the acts contemplated might not be expressly prohibited by law.	*Racially discriminatory contracts are void against public policy.*
		Illegality	If formation or performance of the contract was tortious or illegal when entered into, or if the contract was legal, but subsequently became illegal because of a change in the law, the contract is void.	*Contracts requiring parties to steal goods from warehouses.*

Defenses to Contract Formation

A contract may be unenforceable if there was no mutual assent regarding the fundamentals of the agreement when the contract was formed. If one party can demonstrate that the parties did not reach a meeting of the minds, that party may have a defense to the terms of an otherwise valid contract.

Defense	Definition	Rule
AMBIGUITY/ MISUNDERSTANDING	Where the contract provision is reasonably susceptible to more than one interpretation.	Where an ambiguity exists, a court must look to extrinsic evidence to determine the intent of the parties and the meaning of the terms to determine and whether enough evidence exists to interpret the contract with sufficient certainty to render it enforceable.
MUTUAL MISTAKE	Parties each made a factual error about the meaning of a material term in the contract.	Mutual mistake renders a contract voidable.
UNILATERAL MISTAKE	One party to a contract is mistaken as to the terms or subject matter contained in the contract.	One party's mistake will generally not void the contract and excuse performance under a contract.
MISREPRESENTATION	False statement made by one party to another which has the effect of inducing that party to enter into the contract.	Finding of misrepresentation allows for rescission, and under certain circumstances, damages.
NON-DISCLOSURE	Failure by one party, to disclose a material fact that relates to the subject matter of the contract.	Non-disclosure will generally not excuse a party from contractual obligations. There is no affirmative duty to disclose information unless (1) the parties have a fiduciary relationship, OR (2) one party has special knowledge about a material fact that the other party cannot learn with normal diligence, OR (3) disclosure is necessary to correct a mistake of the other party as to a basic assumption of the contract.

Lack of Capacity Defenses

A contract may be unenforceable as a result of a party's lack of volitional consent or inability to consent as a result of being a member of a protected class.

Defense	Definition	Rule
INFANCY	Infants are people below the age of 18 who the law has deemed incapable of understanding the consequences of incurring binding obligations.	Failure to disaffirm a contract entered into as an infant within a reasonable time of becoming an adult will cause the contract to become binding. Contracts entered into by an infant and an adult are voidable by the infant, but binding on the adult.
MENTAL INCOMPETENCY	A person who is mentally incompetent is an individual whose mental capacity is so deficient that she is incapable of understanding the nature and consequences of a contract.	Contracts entered into by a mentally incompetent person are voidable by such person or can be affirmed by the mentally incompetent person during a lucid interval or upon recovery.
INTOXICATION	A person is intoxicated if, as a result of a substance being consumed, she is incapable of understanding the nature and consequences of a contract.	Contracts entered into by intoxicated people are voidable if the other party had reason to know of the intoxication. The contract can be affirmed by the intoxicated person once she is sober.
DURESS	Illegal coercion, threats or acts that have a powerful influence which preclude a party from exercising free will.	Duress is available as a defense if one party used force or the threat of force or harm to obtain an agreement to contract, but the defense of economic duress in which one party takes advantage of the other's immediate financial need to contract does not qualify as a defense which would void a contract.
UNDUE INFLUENCE	Unfair use of a person's relationship or position to put excessive pressure on another party to enter into a contract, or to agree to certain terms which are unjustly beneficial to the party exercising the influence.	Unlike duress, undue influence does not involve a threat, but rather involves one party taking unfair advantage of the other's weakness or vulnerability. A contract induced by undue influence is voidable by the victim.
FRAUD	A party who enters into a contract based upon false information intentionally provided as a means of coercing the party into entering the contract.	A contract induced by fraud is voidable by the victim.

Defenses to Contractual Enforcement

Once a contract has been formed, the parties may be excused from performance under circumstances in which enforcement of the terms would cause an unfair result.

Defense	Definition	Examples
AGAINST PUBLIC POLICY	A contract will not be enforced if it differs from the basic policies forming the foundation of public laws, even though the acts contemplated might not be expressly prohibited by law.	*Joy and Max agree to live together and orally agree on an arrangement in which Joy will financially support Max so long as Max fixes everything around the house. Courts traditionally have refused to enforce cohabitation agreements on the grounds that they amount to payment for sex.*
ILLEGALITY	If formation or performance of a contract was tortious or criminal when entered into, or if a legal contract becomes illegal because of a change in the law, the parties will be excused from performing their duties under the contract.	*Supermarket enters into a three-year contract with Beer Wholesaler to sell its beer in its supermarkets. After a year, a new law is passed making it illegal to sell alcohol in supermarkets. The contract will become unenforceable because the agreement is now illegal.*
FRUSTRATION OF PURPOSE	If unanticipated events destroy the mutually agreed upon subject matter or purpose of the agreement, the parties will be excused from performing their duties under the contract.	*Beka is a singer. She rents a nightclub for Saturday night so she can host a concert. The morning before the concert, the nightclub's sound system broke. Beka's duty to rent the club is excused because the purpose of the contract was frustrated by an unforeseen event.*
IMPRACTICABILITY	If performance is possible, but infeasible or commercially unrealistic due to unanticipated events, the parties may be excused from performing their duties under the contract.	*Bride contracted with Seamstress to have her wedding dress sewn from silk imported from China. A week after entering into the contract with Seamstress, the U.S. government halted trade with China, causing an immediate shortage in available Chinese silk and a 1000% increase in the price of available silk. Parties will be excused from performance based on commercial impracticability.*
IMPOSSIBILITY	If unanticipated events not caused by the fault of either party make performance objectively impossible, the parties will be excused from performing their duties under the contract.	*A contract states that Beatz, a musician residing in Chicago, will be the rapper that performs at Matt's party in Ohio. The day of the party, Chicago was struck by a snow storm and all flights coming into and leaving Chicago were canceled. Beatz will be excused from performing and Matt will be excused from paying Beatz because performance of the contract is rendered impossible.*
UNCONSCIONABILITY	Contracts in which parties are in an unequal bargaining position, and there is an absence of meaningful choice for one party and unreasonably favorable terms for the other.	*Record Label offered Musician a three year contract. Under the terms of the contract, Record Label earned 80% of profits generated by Musician, and the remaining 20% was paid to Musician. Similar contracts in the industry split profits equally between the record labels and the musicians. During negotiations, Record Label told Musician to take it or leave it, and refused to provide musician time to consult an attorney. Musician entered into the contract. The contract will be voidable at the election of Musician based on the defense of unconscionability.*
STATUTE OF FRAUDS	These contracts will not be enforced unless in writing: (1) promises to marry, (2) contracts that cannot be performed within one year, (3) conveyances of land, (4) sale of goods of $500 or more, (5) agreements to pay the debts of another.	*Lauren agrees to sell Vic her house for $500,000. They orally agree on the terms of the sale. This contract is unenforceable because contracts for the conveyance of real property must be in writing signed by the party to be charged.*

Types of Warranties

A warranty is a promise or guarantee, made by the seller of goods,
that the goods will perform in accordance with the promise.

	Type	Definition	How Warranty Arises	By Whom	Disclaimer
	EXPRESS WARRANTIES	An affirmative promise or guarantee made by seller about the goods, which becomes part of the basis of the bargain.	By affirmation of fact, promise, description, model or sample.	Seller.	Seller may not disclaim an express warranty it has given, but can disclaim or exclude the making of any other express warranties by clear and concise language.
IMPLIED WARRANTIES	Warranty of Title	An implied promise or guarantee that the seller has legal title to the goods, that the transfer is rightful and that there are no liens or encumbrances.	Implicit in every sale unless effectively disclaimed.	Seller.	By specific language or circumstances showing seller does not represent or guarantee title.
	Warranty of Merchantability	An implied promise or guarantee made by a merchant, that the goods are fit for ordinary purposes.	Implicit in every sale by a merchant unless effectively disclaimed.	Merchants only.	By disclaimer mentioning "merchantability" (if disclaimer is written, and must be conspicuous). By inspection or refusal to inspect, where an inspection would reveal the defect.
	Warranty for Fitness for Particular Purpose	A promise or guarantee that the goods are fit for buyer's particular purpose.	(1) Seller must have reason to know of buyer's particular purpose for the goods; (2) Seller must have reason to know of buyer's reliance on seller's skill and knowledge in furnishing the appropriate goods; AND (3) Buyer must, in fact, rely on seller's skill and knowledge.	Merchants only.	By conspicuous written disclaimer.

Discharge of Contracts

If both parties agree, one or both parties can be discharged from their obligations under the contract.

	Definition	Time of Discharge
ACCORD AND SATISFACTION	An accord is an agreement between the parties to a contract, that one party will substitute its contracted duty for another duty in the future, in exchange for the other party's acceptance of that substitution and discharge of the existing duty.	Discharge of the previous duty does not occur until the terms of the accord are performed.
RELEASE	A contract can be discharged by creation of an executed release, which terminates a party's contractual rights, so long as it is supported by consideration.	Discharge occurs when the executed release is delivered.
RESCISSION	So long as neither party has fully performed under a contract, the parties may agree to cancel the contract.	Discharge occurs when the agreement to destroy the contract is made, unless the rescission is subject to the statute of frauds and has to be in writing, in which case discharge occurs when the written rescission is signed.
SUBSTITUTED AGREEMENT	A substituted agreement can be created to replace a previous contract.	Discharge occurs immediately upon replacement of a new agreement, unless the substituted agreement is subject to the statute of frauds and has to be in writing, in which case discharge occurs when the written substituted agreement is signed.
NOVATION	A complete substitution of parties, in which original parties to a contract along with a substitute party, agree to a complete assignment of rights and obligations under the contract to the substitute party and release the original contracting party from any further rights and obligations under the contract.	Discharge occurs upon agreement of all parties to the novation.

Assignment of Rights and Delegation of Duties

	Definition	Parties	Transfer Rules	Parties' Rights and Liabilities	Examples
ASSIGNMENT OF RIGHTS	The transfer of a party's rights under a contract to a third party.	Three Parties: Obligor, Assignor and Assignee. **Obligor** and **Assignor** have a contract under which Assignor has certain rights. Assignor transfers the rights owed to her by Obligor under the contract, to third party **Assignee.**	Assignee may freely assign (transfer) her contractual rights under a contract to a third party, unless: (1) contract prohibits such assignments, OR (2) assignment would substantially change Obligor's duty, OR (3) assignment would substantially change Obligor's risk, OR (4) assignment would diminish the likelihood of Obligor obtaining return performance. **Note:** Rights to money are always assignable, irrespective of any restriction on the ability to assign under the contract.	<u>Assignee v. Obligor</u>: If Obligor fails to provide the rights to which Assignee is entitled, Assignee can sue the Obligor, but is subject to the same defenses the obligor would have against the assignor. <u>Assignee v. Assignor</u>: If Obligor fails to provide the rights to which Assignee is entitled, Assignee will only have rights against Assignor if: (1) the assignment was made for consideration, or (2) Assignee is a creditor.	*Mitch gets a mortgage from Citibank. In return, Mitch agrees to pay Citibank in monthly installments plus interest. Citibank may assign the mortgage to another bank, which, in turn, will have the right to collect Mitch's monthly payments.*
DELEGATION OF DUTIES	The transfer of a party's duties to perform under a contract to a third party.	Three Parties: Obligor, Obligee and Delegate. **Obligor** and **Obligee** have a contract under which Obligor has the duty to perform. Obligor transfers her duty owed to Obligee under the contract, to third party **Delegate,** to perform the contractual obligation instead of Obligor.	Obligor may freely delegate (transfer) her contractual duties to a third party without obligee's consent unless: (1) contract prohibits such delegations, OR (2) duties require a special artistic or professional skill, OR (3) Obligor was originally chosen because of her reputation.	<u>Obligee v. Obligor</u>: If Delegate fails to perform or performs improperly, Obligor will remain liable to Obligee, unless there has been a novation. **Novation:** An agreement between the parties to a contract, to replace an existing party to the contract so that the new party will be liable and the original party's liabilities under the contract are extinguished. <u>Obligee v. Delegate</u>: If Delegate received compensation from Obligor and knows that the performance rendered is for the benefit of a third party, then Obligee will have rights against Delegate as a third party beneficiary to the contract between Obligor and Delegate. If Delegate has not received compensation from Obligor, Obligee has no rights against Delegate.	*Homeowner enters into a contract with Contractor to renovate her kitchen. Contractor may delegate some of her duties under the contract with Homeowner to subcontractors, such as delegating the duty to tile the floor to American Tile Co. and the duty to build and install the cabinets to American Cabinetry.*

Material Breach of Contracts for the Sale of Goods

	Definition	Timing	Standard	Effect
REJECTION	Buyer may reject any non-conforming delivery from Seller so long as the goods deviate in any respect from what is required under the contract.	Before acceptance of the goods.	Sale of goods contracts for a single delivery of goods are subject to the **Perfect Tender Rule:** if the goods or tender of delivery of goods fail *in any respect* to conform to the contract, the buyer can: (1) reject the whole, (2) accept the whole, OR (3) accept any unit or units and reject the rest. Sale of goods contracts for multiple deliveries, or requirements and output contracts are subject to a standard of substantial performance.	Buyer can return goods without penalty.
REVOCATION	After buyer has accepted the goods, if she subsequently discovers a defect, she may be able to revoke her acceptance upon showing that (1) the defect could not be discovered earlier, AND (2) the defect substantially impairs the value of the contract, AND (3) she provides reasonable notice.	After acceptance.	**Substantial Impairment.** Buyer can revoke her acceptance if she can show not just that the goods somehow deviate from the contract terms, but rather that the non-conformity of the goods substantially impairs the value of the goods.	Buyer can return goods and receive a refund.

Anticipatory Repudiation

Anticipatory repudiation is a breach of contract that occurs before performance is due when there is an unequivocal indication that one of the parties will not perform.

Types	Rule	Breach	Examples
BANKRUPTCY	A party's bankruptcy is generally considered to be an anticipatory repudiation, allowing the promisee to make a claim in bankruptcy.	✔	*A manufacturer who is supposed to deliver 1,000 pairs of sunglasses to a store files for Chapter 11. The store can consider this a breach of contract and immediately sue the manufacturer.*
INSISTENCE ON NON-CONTRACTUAL TERMS	A party's insistence on additional terms that are not in the contract is sufficient to be considered an anticipatory repudiation.	✔	*John agrees to sell Gary 400 wine glasses for his restaurant. According to the contract, delivery costs were included in the agreed upon purchase price, however, John keeps telling Gary that he will not deliver the glasses until Gary pays him an additional $100 for delivery. Gary may treat the demand as an anticipatory repudiation and immediately sue John for breach.*
INSOLVENCY	A promisor's actual or apparent insolvency is not in and of itself an anticipatory repudiation, and does not allow the promisee to immediately sue for breach. However, upon learning of an actual or apparent insolvency, the promisee may demand adequate assurances of performance, and if the promisor fails to demonstrate an ability to perform within 30 days of the demand, then an immediate breach of contract action is available.	✘	*A manufacturer agrees to deliver 500 shirts to Shirt Depot. After the contracts are signed, the owner of Shirt Depot reads that the manufacturer was sued by a different company and now owes three million dollars. Shirt Depot cannot sue manufacturer for breach of contract because it assumes the manufacturer is now insolvent and unable to deliver the shirts, but it can demand the manufacturer present a bank statement or some other assurance of its ability to perform within 30 days.*
STATEMENTS	Only an unequivocal refusal to perform contractual duties will be sufficient to be considered an anticipatory repudiation. Expressions of vague doubt about a party's willingness or ability to perform are insufficient.	✔	*Pete agrees to paint Nick's house for $600. While Pete is painting, Nick says, "I hope I'm able to pay you, the stock market is really down." This statement alone is insufficient to constitute an anticipatory repudiation. However, if Nick were to say, "I'm not going to pay you because I lost too much money in the stock market," Pete would be able to sue Nick immediately for breach of contract.*

Remedies in Breach of Contract Cases

In breach of contract disputes, a court generally awards money damages to the injured party. Where money damages are inadequate to compensate the injured party, relief in equity is available.

Types of Remedies	Definition	Examples of Remedies	Definition
REMEDIES AT LAW	A ***monetary*** remedy ordered by a court, to be paid to the injured party as a recourse for a breached contract.	**EXPECTATION DAMAGES**	Expectation damages compensate the non-breaching party for any benefit it would have received had the contract not been breached. The intention is to put the non-breaching party in the position it would have been in if the contract were performed.
		RELIANCE DAMAGES	Reliance damages compensate the non-breaching party for expenses or losses incurred in reasonable reliance on the breached contract.
		RESTITUTION	Restitution damages compensate the non-breaching party by demanding the return of the property or the monetary value of loss.
EQUITABLE RELIEF	A ***non-monetary*** remedy ordered by a court that is obtained when a legal remedy such as money damages, cannot adequately redress the injury.	**SPECIFIC PERFORMANCE**	Specific performance is an order of a court, which requires a party to perform as an alternative to awarding monetary damages.
		INJUNCTION	An injunction is a court order prohibiting a party from doing a particular act.

Monetary Damages Available in Breach of Contract Cases

There are three types of measures that a court can use to determine the amount that a party has been injured as a result of a breached contract.

Type	Definition	Purpose	When Used
EXPECTATION DAMAGES	Expectation damages compensate the non-breaching party for any benefit she would have received had the contract not been breached.	To restore the non-breaching party to the position she would have been in had the contract been fulfilled.	When the amount of damages can be proven with certainty. The amount is measured by the contract price, loss in value, or lost profits.
RELIANCE DAMAGES	Reliance damages compensate the non-breaching party for expenses or losses incurred in reasonable reliance on the terms of the breached contract.	To restore the non-breaching party to the position she would have been in if the contract had not been made.	When it is impossible to accurately measure the benefit the non-breaching party would have received had the contract not been breached. Only used in circumstances in which expectation damages cannot be determined. When the non-breaching party recovers on the theory of quasi contract/promissory estoppel.
RESTITUTION	Restitution damages compensate the non-breaching party by demanding the return of the property or the monetary value of loss.	To prevent unjust enrichment.	When a non-breaching party has partially performed and the amount of restitution is greater than the amount in the contract. When a breaching party has not substantially performed, but is still allowed to recover an amount equal to the benefit that the non-breaching party received.

Criminal Law

	Model Penal Code	The MPC is a scholarly text created to assist state legislatures in updating and standardizing criminal laws to form a comprehensive and coherent body of penal law.

Summaries of Selected Provisions
Below are summaries of selected provisions of the MPC intended as a quick reference to the most frequently tested provisions.

Section	Title	Description
§2.01	Requirement of Voluntariness	Criminal culpability requires a person's conduct to be voluntary.
§2.02	Requirements of Culpability	A person cannot be convicted of an offense unless she acted intentionally, recklessly, or negligently, with respect to each material element of the offense. [§2.02(1)] **Intentional** conduct is done: 　**Purposely:** a conscious goal to engage in certain conduct or cause a certain result. [§2.02(2)(a)(i)]; OR 　**Knowingly:** knowledge that a specific result is virtually certain to occur. [§2.02(2)(b)(ii)] **Recklessly:** Conscious disregard of substantial and unjustified risk. [§2.02(2)(c)] **Negligently:** Substantial and unjustifiable risk of harm is a foreseeable consequence. [§2.02(2)(d)]
§2.03	Causal Relationship Between Conduct and Result	**Specific intent crimes** — result must be the intended purpose of the action. [§2.03 (2)] **Negligent/Reckless crimes** — result must be a foreseeable consequence of the action. [§2.03 (3)] **Strict liability crimes** — result must be a probable consequence of the conduct. [§2.03 (4)]
§2.04	Ignorance or Mistake	Mistake of fact is a defense to specific intent crimes if the mistake negates the mental state essential to the crime charged. [§2.04(1)] Ignorance of the law is generally not a defense to a crime, although the MPC recognizes a narrow exception where: 　i) a person does not know the conduct is illegal; AND 　ii) the statute defining the offense was not published or otherwise reasonably made available prior to the violation. [§2.04(3)(a)]
§2.06	Liability for Conduct of Another	A person is legally accountable for the conduct of another when: 　i) she acts with the kind of culpability sufficient for commission of the offense and causes an innocent person to participate; OR 　ii) she is accountable for such person by law; OR 　iii) she is an accomplice of such person. [§2.06(2)] Accomplice liability if: 　i) with the specific intent to promote or facilitate the crime: 　　a) she solicits another to assist, aid or agree to aid in planning and committing the crime; OR 　　b) fails to make the effort to prevent a crime she is likely responsible for. [§2.06(3)(a)] A person is **not guilty** as an accomplice in the commission of an offense if: 　i) she was the victim; OR 　ii) if her conduct was inevitably incidental to the commission of the crime. [§2.06(6)] A person avoids accomplice liability if she **withdraws** before the commission of the crime; AND 　i) wholly undoes the effect of her prior actions, OR 　ii) alerts law enforcement authorities, or makes other proper efforts to prevent the crime. [§2.06(6)(c)] An accomplice may be convicted of a crime upon proof of its commission by another person, regardless of whether the other person is convicted or prosecuted. [§2.06(7)]

Summaries of Selected Provisions, *continued*

Section	Title	Description
§2.08	Intoxication	Intoxication can be used as a defense if it negates an element of the crime. [§2.08(1)] Voluntary intoxication can be a defense to specific intent crimes, but **not** crimes involving negligence or recklessness since the act of becoming intoxicated may be regarded as negligent or reckless in and of itself. [§2.08(2)] Involuntary intoxication can be a defense to specific intent crimes **and** crimes involving negligence and recklessness.
§2.09	Duress	Duress is the use of force or the threat of force to compel commission of a crime. [§2.09] Duress is an affirmative defense if: 　i) accused was compelled to commit the offense by force or the threat of immediate death or serious injury to herself or another; OR 　ii) a "person of reasonable firmness" would not have been able to resist the coercion. [§2.09(1)]
§210.1	Criminal Homicide	A person is guilty of homicide if she intentionally, recklessly or negligently takes the life of another.
§210.2	Murder	A killing committed intentionally or recklessly manifesting extreme indifference to human life. Extreme indifference to human life is presumed if the accused commits a homicide while committing, attempting to commit, or fleeing from a dangerous felony.
§210.3	Manslaughter	A reckless homicide, or a homicide committed under the influence of extreme mental or emotion disturbance for which there is reasonable explanation or excuse. ** MPC does not distinguish between voluntary and involuntary manslaughter. **
§210.4	Negligent Homicide	Homicide committed negligently; defendant breaches a duty that causes death.
§211.1	Assault	Simple Assault: 　i) intentional or reckless attempt to cause bodily injury to another; OR 　ii) intentional placing of another in fear of imminent, serious, bodily injury; OR 　iii) negligent causing of bodily injury to another with a deadly weapon. [§211.1(1)] Aggravated Assault: 　i) attempt to cause serious bodily injury to another; OR 　ii) intentional or reckless causing of injury with extreme indifference to human life; OR 　iii) attempt to cause, or intentionally causing bodily injury to another with a deadly weapon. [§2.11.1(2)]
§211.2	Reckless Endangering	It is a misdemeanor to recklessly engage in conduct which places, or may place, another in danger of death or serious bodily injury.
§213.1	Rape	Rape: Intentional or reckless sexual intercourse by a male with a female: 　i) under ten years of age; OR 　ii) that is unconscious; OR 　iii) by forcing or threatening imminent death, grievous bodily harm, extreme pain or kidnapping; OR 　iv) induces the victim to become intoxicated such that the victim's ability to control her conduct is substantially impaired. [§213.1(1)]
§213.4	Sexual Assault	A person who has sexual contact with another (not his spouse), or causes such other to have sexual contact with him with knowledge that: 　i) the contact is offensive; OR 　ii) the other person suffers from a mental disease or defect which renders her incapable of appraising the situation; OR 　iii) the other person is unaware that a sexual act is being committed; OR 　iv) the other person is less than ten years of age; OR 　v) the other person's ability to appraise or control her conduct has been substantially impaired by the administration of drugs, intoxicants etc ... without the other person's knowledge for the purpose of preventing resistance; OR 　vi) the other person is less than sixteen years of age, and the actor is at least 4 years older; OR 　vii) the other person is less than twenty one years of age, and the actor is her guardian; OR 　viii) the other person is in custody of the law, or detained in a hospital or other institution and the actor has authority over her.

Summaries of Selected Provisions, *continued*

Section	Title	Description
§ 213.6	Mistake of Age	Not knowing a child's age, or reasonably believing a child to be older than a certain age is not a meritorious defense. [§ 213.6(1)]
§ 3.02	Justification	Conduct reasonably believed to be necessary to avoid harm, if the gravity of the harm sought to be avoided is greater than the crime [§ 3.02(1)] If actor reckless or negligent in causing the harm, the justification defense is unavailable. [§ 3.02(2)]
§ 3.04	Self-Defense	A person is justified in using force upon another if she reasonably believes the force is immediately necessary to protect against the use of force by another, or a threat of rape or kidnapping. [§ 3.04(1)] Deadly force is only justifiable when person reasonably believes such force is immediately necessary to protect against death, serious bodily injury, kidnapping, or rape. [§ 3.04(2)(b)] One may <u>NOT</u> use deadly force if she can safely retreat, unless she is in her own home or office. [§ 3.04(2)(b)(ii)] There is no duty to retreat from one's own home or place of work.

§ 3.05	Use of Force for the Protection of Others	Force is justifiable to protect a third party when:
		   i) it is no more than necessary to protect the third-party, AND
		   ii) under circumstances the third party would have been justified in using force; AND
		   iii) it is reasonably necessary for the third party's protection. [§ 3.05(1)]
		 No duty to retreat unless the complete safety of the third party is assured. [§ 3.05(2)(a)]
		 If the third party would have been required to retreat, the intervenor must attempt to secure the third party's retreat if the intervenor knows the third party can reach complete safety. [§ 3.05(2)(b)]
		 No duty to retreat in the third party's home or place of work to any greater extent than one's own home or place of work. [§ 3.05(2)(c)]

§ 3.06	Use of Force for the Protection of Property	Non-deadly force reasonably believed to be immediately necessary to prevent trespass or the unlawful carrying away of personal property is permissible where:
		   i) the other person's interference with the property is unlawful; AND
		   ii) the intrusion deprived rightful possession of land or property; AND
		   iii) force is immediately necessary, or the taker has no claim of right to possession. [§ 3.06(1)]
		 Actor must request desistance prior to using force, unless there is a reason to believe such request would be futile or result in substantial harm to the property sought to be protected. [§ 3.06(3)(a)]
		 <u>Not justifiable</u> if use of force would expose the trespasser to a substantial danger of serious bodily injury. [§ 3.06(3)(b)]
		 Non-deadly force to **re-enter** land, or **recapture** personal property is permitted if:
		   i) there is reason to believe there is an unlawful deprivation of property, or possessor has no claim of right to possess the property; AND
		   ii) the force is used immediately after taking of the property. [§ 3.06(3)(c)]
		 Deadly force is <u>not justified</u> unless there is reasonable belief of an:
		   i) attempt to deprive a person of a right to possess their dwelling, OR
		   ii) attempt to commit arson, burglary, robbery, felonious theft, or property destruction; AND
		   iii) the other person used or threatens to use deadly force. [§ 3.06(3)(d)]
		 Use of a device to protect property is justified if it:
		   i) is not designed to cause death or serious bodily injury; AND
		   ii) is reasonably used to protect the property from entry by another, AND
		   iii) is customarily used for the purpose of protecting the property; AND
		   iv) reasonable warning is provided of probable use. [§ 3.06(5)(a)]

§ 3.09	Mistake of Law; Reckless or Negligent Use of Justifiable Force	Use of force for self-defense, defense of others, defense of property or for use in law enforcement are **unavailable** when:
		   i) the actor's justification for use of force is unlawful or erroneous, AND
		   ii) her error is due to ignorance or mistaken interpretation of the law. [§ 3.09(1)]

§ 4.01	Mental Disease or Defect	Lack of capacity to appreciate the wrongfulness of conduct, or to conform conduct to the requirements of the law. [§ 4.01(1)] Affirmative defense to criminal liability.

Summaries of Selected Provisions, *continued*

Section	Title	Description
§ 5.01	Attempt	**Attempt:** a person is guilty of an attempt to commit a crime if she: i) acts intentionally with criminal culpability; AND ii) takes a substantial step towards the objective of committing the crime. [§ 5.01(1)] <u>Substantial Step:</u> (1) waiting, searching for, or following the victim; OR (2) seeking to entice the victim to go where crime is to be committed; OR (3) reconnoitering place contemplated for commission of crime; OR (4) unlawfully entering place where crime is to be committed; OR (5) possessing materials to be employed in the commission of the crime; OR (6) collecting or fabricating materials to be used in the commission near where crime is to be committed; OR (7) soliciting an innocent agent to engage in conduct constituting an element of the crime. [§ 5.01(2)] A person may be convicted of attempt even if a crime was not committed or attempted by another if: i) purpose of conduct was to aid another in the commission of the offense, AND ii) assistance would have made her an accomplice if the crime had been committed or attempted. [§ 5.01(3)] Withdrawal/Abandonment is a defense if: i) voluntary; AND ii) complete. [§ 5.01(4)]
§ 5.02	Solicitation	A person is guilty of solicitation if: i) specific intent to promote or facilitate commission of a crime; AND ii) she commands, encourages or requests another to engage in conduct constituting the crime or an attempt. [§ 5.02(1)] Withdrawal/Abandonment is a defense if conspirator: i) makes a complete and voluntarily renunciation of criminal intent; AND ii) persuades or prevents commission of the crime. [§ 5.02(3)]
§ 5.03	Conspiracy	A person is guilty of conspiracy if there is an intentional agreement with another to commit, attempt, plan or solicit a crime. [§ 5.03(1)] Proof of an overt act required for misdemeanors or felonies in the third degree. [§ 5.03(5)] Withdrawal/Abandonment is a defense if: i) voluntary renunciation of the crime; AND ii) prevents commission of that crime. [§ 5.03(6)]

Theoretical Purposes of Criminal Punishment
Philosophy of Criminal Punishment.

Theories	Definition	Goals	Definition
UTILITARIANISM	Theory that criminals are less likely to commit crimes because they want to avoid punishment; punishment is imposed for the good of society by preventing and minimizing crime. The basis of the theory is the belief that potential criminals will balance the likelihood of success of their crime with the severity of the punishment.	**SPECIAL DETERRENCE**	Punishment of an individual may prevent *that* individual from committing future crime.
		GENERAL DETERRENCE	Punishment of an individual may deter others from committing similar crimes for fear of similar punishment.
RETRIBUTIVISM	A theory of justice that considers punishment a morally acceptable response to crime. Punishment as a means to avenge morally culpable behavior, irrespective of whether the punishment reduces crime.	**INCAPACITATION**	Incarceration removes the opportunities for the incarcerated to harm society.
		RETRIBUTION	Incarceration and criminal punishment are a means of revenge.
DENUNCIATION	A theory that punishment is a demonstration of societal condemnation of a crime. The punishment is a means of educating a criminal that society regards specific conduct as improper, and achieving a means of societal retribution.	**REHABILITATION AND REFORMATION**	The criminal justice system through incarceration and other forms of punishment provides a means of education and reform such that individuals are retrained to follow social norms, and criminal behavior is deterred.

Elements of a Crime

Most crimes have five elements: (1) mens rea, (2) actus reus, (3) concurrence, (4) causation, AND (5) harmful result.

	Definition	Categories	Definition
MENS REA	The legally prescribed mental state of a criminal before or during the commission of a crime.	**INTENTIONALLY**	**Purposely:** goal to engage in certain conduct or cause a certain result. **Knowingly:** knowledge that a specific result is certain to occur as a result of conduct.
		RECKLESSLY	Conscious disregard of substantial and unjustifiable risk.
		NEGLIGENTLY	Inadvertent disregard of a substantial and unjustifiable risk exists or will result.
ACTUS REUS	The physical commission of a crime.	**COMMISSION**	Voluntary action.
		OMISSION	Failure to act will be criminal if: (1) there is a legal duty to act; AND (2) the person is aware of the duty.
CONCURRENCE	Presence of mental culpability *AND* physical act required. There can be no criminal liability for the crime unless it can be shown that the accused's conduct was a cause-in-fact of the prohibited result.		
CAUSATION	The act must actually and proximately cause the harm.	**PROXIMATE**	Action that foreseeably causes harm without the intervention of independent or unforeseeable causes.
		ACTUAL	Action that directly causes the harm.
HARMFUL RESULT	Injury.		

Comparison Chart	The Common Law is the body of law created by judicial decisions and custom, and enforced in the absence of a relevant statute. The Model Penal Code (MPC) is a scholarly text created to help state legislatures standardize penal laws to form a comprehensive and coherent body of criminal law.

Mens Rea
The legally prescribed mental state of a criminal before or during the commission of a crime.

	Model Penal Code	Common Law
INTENT	**General Intent:** a person who acts with the intent to perform an action, but without the intent to cause a precise harm or result. General intent is objective, and applies a reasonable person standard. **Specific Intent:** intent to engage in the crime, or to achieve a specific harm or result. Specific intent is subjective and depends on what the person who committed the crime desired to accomplish.	The MPC does not distinguish between general and specific intent, and instead uses levels of culpability. **Purposely:** the conscious goal to engage in certain conduct or cause a certain result. [§ 2.02(2)(a)(i)] **Knowingly:** knowledge that a specific result is certain to occur as a result of conduct. [§ 2.02(2)(b)(ii)] **Recklessly:** conscious disregard of a substantial and unjustified risk of harm that exists, or will result from her conduct. [§ 2.02(2)(c)] **Negligently:** inadvertent disregard of a substantial and unjustifiable risk of harm that exists, or will result from her conduct. [§ 2.02(2)(d)]
STRICT LIABILITY CRIMES	Crimes not requiring a state of mind (*i.e. statutory rape; bigamy*).	MPC limits strict liability crimes to violations for which the resulting penalty can be a fine or forfeiture, but not incarceration. Strict liability is unrecognized for felonies or misdemeanors.

Actus Reus: "Act" Exceptions
Actus reus is a physical act that causes harm, but there are a few exceptions.

Duty	Rule	Examples
HYPNOSIS	The Model Penal Code recognizes acts committed while a person is hypnotized as being involuntary, and therefore NOT subject to criminal liability.	*Sam goes to a hypnotist to help him quit smoking. The hypnotist puts Sam into a trance. While in a hypnotic state, Sam punches the hypnotist. Sam will not be found criminally liable for the hypnotist's injuries because his actions were not voluntary.*
POSSESSION	Mere possession can constitute an "act" even if there is no bodily movement.	*By having marijuana in his pocket, Jeremy can be criminally liable, notwithstanding the fact that he neither acted to sell it or smoke it.*
REFLEX OR CONVULSION	A criminal act committed as a result of an involuntary reflex or a convulsion will not give rise to criminal liability, unless the actor knew she was subject to such reflex or convulsion, and proceeded to put herself in a position where she could harm another.	*Adam forcefully strikes Melissa while having a seizure. Although Adam has committed a battery, he will not be found criminally liable because his actions were not voluntary.* *Alternatively, if Adam drove a car knowing he suffered from seizures and hit Melissa while having a seizure driving the vehicle, he would be criminally responsible for Melissa's injuries.*
SELF-INDUCED STATE	An involuntary act committed as a result of a voluntary act which alters a person's state of mind, may result in criminally liable.	*Nick takes cough medicine he knows causes drowsiness. After taking the medicine, he drives to a friend's house and falls asleep while driving, thereby killing a pedestrian. Although Nick's act of falling asleep was involuntary, he voluntarily took the cough medicine before operating the car and therefore he will be found criminally liable for the pedestrian's death.*
UNCONSCIOUS STATE OR ASLEEP	Acts committed while a person is in an unconscious state or asleep are not considered voluntary, and will not result in criminal liability unless the person knew she might become unconscious or fall asleep, and still voluntarily put herself in a position where she could cause harm to another.	*While sleep walking, Sue punched her husband. Sue will not be liable for battery since her acts were involuntarily committed while she was asleep.*
UNFORESEEABLE CONSEQUENCES	Acts which result in an unforeseeable consequence will generally not result in criminal culpability.	*Dave and Doug are wrestling in the living room. Dave pushes Doug, and he falls back onto Mandy, who, in turn, becomes startled, has a heart attack and dies. Mandy's death was an unforeseeable result of Dave having pushed Doug. Dave will not be criminally liable for Mandy's death.*

Actus Reus: "Omission" Exceptions

Actus reus is an act that causes harm. Generally, a person has no legal duty to act to prevent harm to another, unless it falls within an exception sufficient to constitute the actus reus element of a crime.

Duty	Definition	Examples
CONTRACTUAL	Contracts may create a duty obligating a person to act.	Nurse enters into a contract with a hospital to care for patients within the hospital; her failure to help or care for a patient that results in harm to that patient may subject the nurse to criminal liability.
CREATION OF PERIL	An affirmative duty to prevent harm when a person creates a dangerous condition.	On a camping trip, Scott set up a trap to catch a bear. He hid the trap under some leaves close to his campsite and failed to warn the other visitors at the campsite. Not seeing the trap, a guest from the campsite walked into the trap, causing injuries to her legs and feet. Scott was subject to an affirmative duty to protect those he put in a dangerous situation with the trap, and his failure to do so will subject him to criminal liability.
SPECIAL RELATIONSHIP	Relationship that includes a legal obligation to protect (*i.e. parent/child; emergency worker/public, husband/wife, employer/employee*).	Parents' failure to provide adequate clothing or nourishment to their child may result in criminal liability.
STATUTORY	Obligation created by statute.	New York State income earners are obligated to pay New York State income tax. Mark works in New York, but refuses to pay his taxes. Mark's failure to pay his taxes is a crime.
VOLUNTARY ASSISTANCE	Rendering assistance to a victim in need creates a duty to exercise reasonable care in providing such assistance; failure to do so will result in criminal liability.	Frank is drowning and he screams for help. Aaron runs onto the dock and begins to assist Frank by throwing a rope to pull him in. While pulling the rope onto which Frank is hanging, Aaron realizes he is late for an appointment and abandons the rescue, thereby causing Frank to drown. Although Aaron was under no legal obligation to rescue Frank, his failure to exercise reasonable care after having initiated the rescue will subject Aaron to criminal liability.

Comparison Chart

The Common Law is the body of law created by judicial decisions and custom, and enforced in the absence of a relevant statute. The Model Penal Code (MPC) is a scholarly text created to help state legislatures standardize penal laws to form a comprehensive and coherent body of criminal law.

Causation

Most crimes have five elements: (1) mens rea, (2) actus reus, (3) concurrence, (4) causation, and (5) harmful injury.

	Common Law	Model Penal Code
ACTUAL CAUSATION	There can be no criminal liability for the crime unless it can be shown that the accused's conduct was a direct cause of the prohibited result. Actual causation includes: (1) actions that are one of several sources causing injury; (2) actions that are taken in conjunction with others to cause the victim harm; OR (3) actions that accelerate the injury.	Actual causation under MPC is the same as under the common law. An accused will be treated as having caused the crime unless the manner in which it occurred was accidental or too remote to have a just bearing on the accused's liability. [§ 2.03(1)(a)]
PROXIMATE CAUSATION	The proximate cause of a crime is an act that causes a *foreseeable* harm. If there is an intervening cause after the misconduct, the intervening cause may terminate the accused's liability if it interferes with the direct link to the harm. Criminal liability will not be avoided if the intervening cause was foreseeable.	MPC determines whether probable cause exists by considering the mens rea. The accused will be treated as having caused the crime if the harm that actually occurred was not accidental or too remote from that which was the accused designed or contemplated. [§ 2.03(2)(b), (3)(c)]

Inchoate Crimes
Offenses committed prior to and in preparation for what may be a more serious offense.

	Definition	Mens Rea	Actus Reus	Legal Tests/Rules	Types	Merge	Is Withdrawal a Defense?
ATTEMPT	An incomplete effort to commit a crime.	An individual must possess the specific intent to achieve a criminal objective AND perform acts that are proximate to the completion of the crime.	**Objective Approach:** requires an act come extremely close to the commission of a crime and distinguishes between planning and actually purchasing materials. Focuses on the danger posed by a person's act. **Subjective Approach:** focuses on a person's intent rather than acts and on the danger to society presented by a person who possesses a criminal intent.	**Last Step Approach:** (Common Law) attempt only occurred following completion of the final step required for commission of a crime. **Substantial Step Test:** (Model Penal Code) actor must take a clear step towards commission of a crime. **Physical Proximity Test:** (Modern) attempt occurs when act is "dangerously close" to completion of a crime.	**Complete (but imperfect):** person takes every act required to commit a crime, but fails. **Incomplete:** person abandons or is prevented from completing a crime.	✔	**Common Law:** No **Model Penal Code:** Yes provided: 1) voluntary; AND 2) complete cancellation of plan to commit crime. [5.01(4)]
CONSPIRACY	An agreement between two or more people to commit a crime.	Specific intent to achieve the object of the agreement; AND actual agreement. **Plurality Requirement:** two or more people intentionally enter into an agreement with intent to achieve the crime. **Bilateral Approach:** charge of conspiracy against one conspirator will fail if the other conspirator lacks mens rea. **Unilateral Approach:** (Model Penal Code) examines whether and individual agreed to enter into conspiracy, rather than whether people simply entered into an agreement.	**Common Law:** intentionally entering into an agreement to commit a crime is sufficient to constitute conspiracy. **Model Penal Code:** intentionally entering into an agreement AND an overt act.	**Pinkerton Rule:** person is guilty of all criminal acts committed by one of the conspirators in furtherance of the conspiracy, regardless of whether the person aided or abetted or was even aware of the offense, provided the criminal act was foreseeable and in furtherance of the conspiracy. **Wharton's Rule:** prohibits the prosecution of two people for conspiracy to commit a particular crime when the crime necessitates two persons.	**Chain Conspiracy:** communication and cooperation by individuals linked together in a vertical chain to achieve the criminal objective. **Wheel Conspiracy:** single person or group that serves as a hub or common core connecting other conspirators.	✘	**Common Law:** No **Model Penal Code:** Yes provided: (1) voluntary; AND (2) renounce participation in conspiracy to other members of the conspiracy; OR (3) notify law enforcement. [5.03 (6)]

Inchoate Crimes, *continued*

Offenses committed prior to and in preparation for what may be a more serious offense.

	Definition	Mens Rea	Actus Reus	Legal Tests/Rules	Types	Merge	Is Withdrawal a Defense?
SOLICITATION	An effort to persuade another person to commit a crime by commanding, hiring or encouraging them to commit that crime.	Specific intent that another individual commit the actual crime.	An affirmative effort to persuade another to commit a crime. A statement justifying or expressing hope that crime will be committed is insufficient; there must be an effort at persuading the person to commit the crime.	Crime is considered complete at the moment the statement requesting another to commit the crime is made.	N/A	✔	**Common Law:** No **Model Penal Code:** Yes provided: (1) voluntary; *AND* (2) prevents commission of the crime [**5.02**].

Comparison Chart	The Common Law is the body of law created by judicial decisions and custom, and enforced in the absence of a relevant statute. The Model Penal Code (MPC) is a scholarly text created to help state legislatures standardize penal laws to form a comprehensive and coherent body of criminal law.

Attempt

	Common Law	Model Penal Code
RULE	Attempt occurs when a person, with the intent to commit an offense, has gone beyond mere preparation toward the commission of that offense.	Attempt occurs when an act committed is a strong demonstration of the person's criminal purpose, constituting a ***substantial step*** in the commission of the crime. [§ 5.01(1)(c)]
TYPES	**Imperfect Attempt:** occurs when a person performs all of the acts that she set out to do, but fails to achieve the criminal goal. **Incomplete Attempt:** person does some of the acts necessary to achieve the criminal goal, but quits or is prevented from achieving the criminal goal.	No differentiation between types of attempt.
TESTS	**Last Act Test:** attempt occurs when the person has performed the last proximate act before the completion of the crime. **Physical Proximity Test:** attempt requires conduct that is close to the completion of the crime. **Dangerous Proximity Test:** attempt requires the person's likelihood of success to be great. **Probable Desistance Test:** attempt occurs if a person reached a point where it is unlikely she would have voluntarily desisted from her effort to commit the crime. **Unequivocality Test:** attempt occurs when a person's conduct unambiguously manifests criminal intent.	**Substantial Step Test:** A person is guilty of an attempt to commit a crime if, acting with the kind of culpability otherwise required for the crime, she: (1) purposely engaged in acts that would constitute the crime if the circumstances were as she believed them to be, OR (2) does or fails to do something with the purpose of causing or with the belief that it will cause a resulting crime, OR (3) purposely does or fails to do something that under the believed circumstances, is an act or omission constituting a substantial step in the criminal plan. [§ 5.01(1)]
WITHDRAWAL	Abandonment is not a defense, even if it is voluntary.	An accused can avoid criminal liability by proving that her abandonment was voluntary and complete, and the commission of the crime is prevented. [§ 5.01(4)]

Comparison Chart

The Common Law is the body of law created by judicial decisions and custom, and enforced in the absence of a relevant statute. The Model Penal Code is a scholarly text created to help state legislatures standardize penal laws to form a comprehensive and coherent body of criminal law.

Conspiracy

	Common Law	Model Penal Code
RULE	Intent and an agreement between two or more people to commit a crime.	A person is guilty of conspiring with another person(s) to commit a crime if she: (1) agrees with such person(s) that one or more of them will commit the crime or make an attempt or solicitation to commit such crime; OR (2) agrees to help the other person(s) in the planning or commission of such crime, or in an attempt or solicitation of such crime. [§ 5.03(1)]
TYPES	**Wheel Conspiracy:** exists when there is a shared criminal purpose among a group which includes a central figure or group ("hub") that participates in illegal activities with each of the conspirators ("spokes"), but the conspirators only deal with the central figure, and not each other. **Chain Conspiracy:** all parties must have similar interests which cannot be accomplished unless each party successfully performs its part of the arrangement.	N/A
OVERT ACT	The crime of conspiracy is complete upon agreement. No overt act is necessary.	Overt act required for misdemeanors or felonies in the third degree. [§ 5.03(5)]
CONSPIRATORIAL	To commit unlawful acts; OR lawful acts by unlawful means.	The objective of the agreement must be to commit a crime(s).
PLURALITY REQUIREMENT	**Bilateral Approach:** charge of conspiracy against one conspirator will fail if the other lacked the requisite mens rea for the crime being committed.	**Unilateral Approach:** A person is guilty of conspiracy with another person if she agrees with the other person to commit an offense irrespective of whether the other person had the requisite intent. [§ 5.03(1)]
ABANDONMENT	No withdrawal defense to crime of conspiracy. Although liability for subsequent crimes committed by co-conspirators can be avoided.	Withdrawal defense recognized provided: (1) voluntary; AND (2) renounce participation in conspiracy to other members of the conspiracy; OR (3) notify law enforcement. [§ 5.03(6)]
EXCEPTIONS	**Wharton's Rule:** if two people enter into an agreement to commit an offense that by definition requires the participation of two, they cannot be prosecuted for conspiracy.	No Wharton's Rule.

Relationships Between Co-Conspirators

A conspiracy is an agreement between two or more people to do either an unlawful act or a lawful act by unlawful means.

Type	Definition	Examples
WHEEL CONSPIRACIES	Shared criminal purpose among a group, which includes a central figure or group ("hub") that participates in illegal activities with each of the conspirators ("spokes"), but the conspirators only deal with the central figure, and not each other.	*A madam runs a brothel and employs multiple prostitutes. Even if all of those individuals do not know each other, they are aware of the existence of one another, and each deals separately and directly with the madam, but not one another.*
CHAIN CONSPIRACIES	Parties must have a similar interest which cannot be accomplished unless each party successfully performs its part of the arrangement.	*A group of people participates in a drug ring from Mexico into the United States. Victor grows the marijuana plants on his farm. Mark dries and packages the marijuana, and then sells it in bulk to Todd. Todd separates the marijuana into small packages and distributes the drugs to four friends who sell it on the streets. Each participant in this conspiracy is required to achieve the criminal objective of selling marijuana, and while each knows the next person in the chain, they may not all know all of the other participants.*
PARTIES WHO ENTER LATE	A party who enters a conspiracy in progress will be liable for those acts for which she is on notice and acknowledges.	*Andrew owns an electronics store. He buys stolen televisions and laptops from Jodi and Jim. Andrew is liable for conspiring to sell stolen electronics, but not for the thefts themselves.*
PARTIES WHO LEAVE EARLY	A party who leaves a conspiracy before it is completed will be liable for the subsequent acts committed, if such acts were within the confines of the original agreement.	*Pete, James and Mick decide to rob a store. Pete is in charge of getting the masks and the gun and James is in charge of driving the get away car. If Pete obtains the supplies, and gives them to Mick before deciding he would abandon the conspiracy, he will still be liable for the robbery.*

Comparison Chart

The Common Law is the body of law created by judicial decisions and custom, and enforced in the absence of a relevant statute. The Model Penal Code is a scholarly text created to help state legislatures standardize penal laws to form a comprehensive and coherent body of criminal law.

Solicitation

	Common Law	Model Penal Code
RULE	Solicitation occurs when one purposefully or intentionally requires, invites, hires, or encourages another to commit a criminal act regardless of whether the other person accepts.	A person is guilty of solicitation if: (1) with specific intent to promote or facilitate the commission of a crime, (2) she commands, encourages or requests another person to engage in conduct that would constitute the crime, or an attempt to commit that crime, with the purpose of promoting or facilitating its commission. [§ 5.02(1)]
RELATIONSHIP OF THE PARTIES	Solicitation will not be found to have occurred in situations where the soliciting party intended to commit the crime herself, but needed help from another person.	Relationship between the parties need not be that of an accomplice and a perpetrator.
WITHDRAWAL/ RENUNCIATION	The offense is complete at the time the solicitation is made, and thus, neither withdrawal nor renunciation are defenses.	Withdrawal/renunciation are affirmative defenses if: (1) there is complete and voluntarily renunciation of the crime; AND (2) the commission of the crime is prevented. [§ 5.02(3)]

Accomplice Liability

A person may be held liable for the conduct of another if she intentionally assists another in committing an offense.

Actor	Act Committed	Liability
PRINCIPAL	Person who commits the crime, or who causes an innocent person to commit the crime.	Principal is liable for the crime itself.
ACCOMPLICE	Person who intentionally helps, advises or encourages the principal to commit the crime.	Accomplice is liable for the crime that the principal was advised or encouraged to commit, and all other foreseeable crimes.
ACCESSORY AFTER THE FACT	Person who intentionally aids a person who has completed the commission of a felony.	Person <u>not</u> liable for the crime itself, but is liable for the lesser charge of being an accessory after the fact.

<table>
<tr>
<td rowspan="2">
Comparison Chart
</td>
<td colspan="2">The Common Law is the body of law created by judicial decisions and custom, and enforced in the absence of a relevant statute. The Model Penal Code is a scholarly text created to help state legislatures standardize penal laws to form a comprehensive and coherent body of criminal law.</td>
</tr>
</table>

Accomplice Liability (Complicity)

	Common Law	Model Penal Code
RULE	A person is guilty of an offense if she had the requisite mental state necessary for the crime committed and she intentionally aided or encouraged another to commit the crime.	A person is guilty of an offense if it is committed by her own conduct or by the conduct of another for whom she is legally accountable. [§ 2.06(1)]
EXCEPTIONS	**Innocent Instrumentality Doctrine** states that a person cannot be tried as an accomplice if she is a child, insane, or coerced into assisting the principal because such individuals are incapable of forming the requisite intent.	MPC has adopted the **Innocent Instrumentality Doctrine.**
PARTIES	**Principal in the First Degree:** a person who, with the requisite mental state for the commission of the crime, actually commits the crime herself or commits the crime through the use of an innocent person or instrumentality. **Principal in the Second Degree:** a person who intentionally assisted in, incited or abetted the commission of the crime and was actually or constructively present with the principal at the time of the crime. **Accessory Before the Fact:** a person who solicits, counsels, commands, assists or encourages the principal in the first degree to commit the crime, but is not actually or constructively present with the principal at the time of the crime. **Accessory After the Fact:** a person who receives, comforts or assists another who she knows has committed a crime, in order to help the other person avoid arrest, trial or conviction.	MPC eliminated the distinction between principals and accessories.
LIABILITY	Common law has adopted the **Natural and Probable Consequences Doctrine,** which states that an accomplice may be convicted of any offense she intentionally solicited, assisted, aided or abetted the principal in committing, as well as, any acts that were a natural and probable consequence of the crime. Accomplice can be convicted of a more serious crime than the principal.	MPC has rejected the Natural and Probable Consequences Doctrine. An accomplice may only be convicted for acts that she intentionally aided, abetted, or encouraged, and not for an act that was a natural and probable consequence of the crime.
WITHDRAWAL	One who has intentionally solicited, assisted, aided or abetted another prior to the commission of a crime may withdraw and avoid liability as an accomplice. Common Law recognizes withdrawal as a defense provided the events are stoppable, and there is communication of the renunciation to the perpetrator.	MPC recognizes withdrawal provided actions are taken to eliminate the effectiveness of the prior assistance, AND prevent commission of the crime or provide timely warning to law enforcement.

Defenses and Punishments for Inchoate Crimes

Inchoate crimes are offenses committed prior to and in preparation for what may be a more serious offense.

	Definition	Completion	Defenses			Punishments
			Factual Impossibility	**Legal Impossibility**	**Withdrawal**	
ATTEMPT	An effort to commit a crime.	The offense is complete when the person has gone beyond preparation with the required intent.	The fact that it would have been impossible to complete the attempted crime is no defense.	Even if the person has gone beyond preparation with the requisite intent, if the act is not illegal, there can be no criminal liability.	**Common Law:** No defense **Model Penal Code:** Yes provided: (1) Voluntary; AND (2) Commission of the crime is prevented. **[5.01 (4)]**	Conviction of attempt.
CONSPIRACY	An agreement between two or more people to commit a crime.	Under **common law**, the offense is complete at the time the agreement is made. Under the **Model Penal Code**, an overt act is required.	The fact that it would have been impossible to complete the crime conspired to is no defense.	The fact that one party is incapable of agreeing is a defense to conspiracy under common law. The fact that one party is incapable of conspiring is not a defense to the other conspirator under MPC.	**Common Law:** No defense **Model Penal Code:** Yes provided: (1) Voluntary; AND (2) Renounce participation in conspiracy to other members of the conspiracy; OR Notify law enforcement. **[5.03(6)]**	Can be convicted of conspiracy <u>AND</u> the principal crime.
SOLICITATION	An effort to persuade another to commit a crime by commanding, hiring, or encouraging them.	The offense is complete at the time the solicitation is made.	The fact that it would have been impossible to complete the crime is no defense once solicitation has occurred.	Legal impossibility is a defense where the person committing the solicitation believes they are soliciting another to perform a criminal act, but the act solicited is NOT, in fact, criminal. Legal impossibility is NOT a defense where solicitation could not have been successful because it was impossible for the individual solicited to commit the crime (*i.e.* *soliciting an officer*).	**Common Law:** No defense **Model Penal Code:** Yes provided: (1) Voluntary; AND (2) The commission of the crime is prevented. **[§ 5.02(3)]**	**Common Law:** solicitation merges with crime, and thus punishment is for solicitation <u>OR</u> the principal offense. **Model Penal Code:** solicitation does NOT merge with crime, and thus punishment can be for solicitation <u>AND</u> the principal offense.

Classification of Crimes
Crimes are classified into three groups: (1) crimes against habitation,
(2) crimes against property, or (3) crimes against the person.

Crime	Common Law Definition	Against
ARSON	The malicious burning of the dwelling house of another.	Habitation.
ASSAULT	The intentional creation of apprehension of imminent bodily injury in another; attempted battery.	Person.
BATTERY	The unlawful use of force against another resulting in offensive touching or injury; a completed assault.	Person.
BURGLARY	The breaking and entering, of a dwelling of another, at night, with intent to commit a felony inside.	Habitation.
EMBEZZLEMENT	Fraudulent conversion of the property of another, by a custodian in possession of the property.	Property.
FALSE IMPRISONMENT	Unlawful confinement of another without consent.	Person.
FALSE PRETENSES	Conveyance of title to property to another in reliance on an intentional misrepresentation made with the intent to defraud.	Property.
FELONY MURDER	Homicide that occurs during the course of an inherently dangerous felony, or in immediate flight therefrom.	Person.
INVOLUNTARY MANSLAUGHTER	Unintentional homicide that results from criminal negligence.	Person.
KIDNAPPING	Unlawful confinement of another without consent, AND movement or concealment of the victim.	Person.
LARCENY	Unlawful taking of the personal property of another without consent and with the intent to permanently deprive.	Property.
MURDER	Homicide with malice aforethought.	Person.
RAPE	Unlawful sexual intercourse with a female, by a male other than her husband, by use of force, threat of force, or against her will.	Person.
ROBBERY	Unlawful taking of the personal property of another with force, and without consent and with the intent to permanently deprive the owner of such property.	Property.
VOLUNTARY MANSLAUGHTER	Homicide provoked by passion in which there is insufficient time for the actor to calm down.	Person.

Common Law State of Mind Classifications of Crimes

Common law crimes can be grouped into one of three states of mind.

	Definition	Mens Rea	Analysis	Examples	
GENERAL INTENT CRIMES	A person who acts with general intent intends to engage in the act that causes harm, but does not necessarily intend the precise harm or result.	Acted with a general awareness.	General intent is objective, so a reasonable person standard is applied.	*Battery.* *False imprisonment.* *Kidnapping.*	*Rape.* *Arson.*
SPECIFIC INTENT CRIMES	A person who acts with specific intent intends to engage in the crime in order to achieve a specific harm or result.	Acted intentionally.	Specific intent is subjective and depends on what the person who committed the crime desired to do.	*Attempt.* *Burglary.* *Conspiracy.* *Embezzlement.*	*Forgery.* *Assault.* *Larceny.* *Solicitation.*
STRICT LIABILITY CRIMES	No mens rea is needed for strict liability crimes because the same injury would result whether or not it was intended.	Mental state irrelevant.	Bright line rule. No analysis needed.	*Public welfare offenses (i.e. selling liquors to a minor).* *Statutory rape.* *Bigamy (in some jurisdictions).*	

Offenses Against Habitation

Crimes are classified into three groups: (1) crimes against habitation, (2) crimes against property, or (3) crimes against the person. While common law elements continue to provide the foundation that defines these crimes, modern courts have updated many of the common law definitions.

	Definition	Elements	Modern Courts
ARSON	The malicious burning of the dwelling of another.	(1) malice, (2) dwelling of another, (3) burning.	Most modern statutes have done away with the requirement that arson can only be committed in a dwelling. Most modern statutes allow for arson to be committed in a person's own dwelling, as well as, buildings that are not dwellings. Most modern statutes have eliminated the requirement that actual burning take place; the starting of a fire with the intent of damaging or destroying the structure is sufficient. Some modern statutes have expanded the definition of arson to include explosions. Some jurisdictions have introduced "arson with intent to defraud an insurer" as a separate offense.
BURGLARY	The breaking and entering of the dwelling of another in the nighttime with the intent to commit a felony.	(1) actual or constructive force used of to gain entry, (2) entering, (3) dwelling of another, (4) at night, (5) with intent to commit a felony at the time entry.	Burglary is a felony at common law and remains a felony. Most modern statutes have abandoned the requirement that entry be by "breaking" and have substituted "unlawful entry or remaining without consent". Most modern statutes have abandoned the requirement that the burglarized place be a dwelling, and include all buildings. Most modern statutes have abandoned the "at night" requirement, and recognize burglary as a crime that can occur at any time of day. Many jurisdictions have introduced "aggravated burglary" as a separate offense that is punished more harshly. This can include burglary of an inhabited dwelling, burglary involving assault upon a person, or burglary with a dangerous weapon.

Offenses Against Property

Crimes are classified into three groups: (1) crimes against habitation, (2) crimes against property, or (3) crimes against the person. Some crimes against property require title to pass as an element of the crime.

	Definition	Elements	Does Title Pass?
EMBEZZLEMENT	Fraudulent conversion of the property of another, by a custodian in possession of the property.	(1) Fraudulent conversion of property, (2) belonging to another, (3) by a custodian of the property.	✘
FALSE PRETENSES	Conveyance of title to property to another in reliance on an intentional misrepresentation made with the intent to defraud.	(1) Acquisition of title to property, (2) belonging to another, (3) by intentional false statement, fraud or misrepresentation, (4) with intent to deceive the victim.	✔
LARCENY	Unlawfully taking of the personal property of another without consent, and with the intent to permanently deprive her of it.	(1) Taking personal property, (2) belonging to another, (3) carrying it away, (4) by trespass, (5) with the intent to permanently deprive the victim of the property.	✘
ROBBERY	Unlawfully taking of the personal property of another by force and without consent, and with the intent to permanently deprive the victim of it.	(1) Taking personal property, (2) belonging to another, (3) from the victim's person or in her presence, (4) by force or intimidation, (5) with the intent to permanently deprive the victim of the property.	✘

Comparison Chart	The Common Law is the body of law created by judicial decisions and custom, and enforced in the absence of a relevant statute. The Model Penal Code is a scholarly text created to help state legislatures standardize the penal law to form a comprehensive and coherent body of criminal law.

Property Crimes

	Common Law	Model Penal Code
CLASSIFICATION	Property crimes are separate crimes under common law.	MPC classifies "theft" as: (1) theft by unlawful taking and disposition, (2) theft by deception, OR (3) theft by extortion.
CRIMES	Embezzlement is not a crime under common law. **Larceny:** Unlawfully taking of the personal property of another without consent, and with the intent to permanently deprive the victim of it.	**Theft by Unlawful Taking and Disposition:** A person is guilty of theft if she unlawfully takes, or exercises unlawful control over, movable property of another with purpose to deprive the victim thereof or if she unlawfully transfers immovable property of another or any interest therein with purpose to benefit herself or another not entitled thereto. [§ 223.2]
	Larceny by Trick: Obtaining the property of another as a result of an intentional false statement, fraud or misrepresentation. **False Pretenses:** Conveyance of title to property of another as a result of an intentionally false statement, fraud or misrepresentation.	**Theft by Deception:** A person has committed theft by deception if she creates or reinforces a false impression regarding the value of property. [§ 223.2]
	Extortion: Improper collection of an unlawful fee by an officer acting in her official capacity.	**Theft by Extortion:** A person has committed theft by extortion if she obtains another's property by threatening to inflict bodily injury on someone; threatening to commit another criminal offense; threatening to accuse someone of a criminal offense; threatening to expose secrets to embarrass someone or tarnish her business reputation; threatening to take or withhold action as an official; threatening to bring about or continue a strike, boycott, or other unofficial, collective action; threatening to testify or refuse to testify about another's legal claim or defense; or threatening to inflict other harm. [§ 223.2]

Comparison Chart	The Common Law is the body of law created by judicial decisions and custom, and enforced in the absence of a relevant statute. The Model Penal Code is a scholarly text created to help state legislatures standardize the penal law to form a comprehensive and coherent body of criminal law.

Larceny

	Common Law	Model Penal Code
DEFINITION	Unlawfully taking the personal property of another without consent, and with the intent to permanently deprive the victim of it.	A person is guilty of "theft" if she unlawfully takes, or exercises unlawful control over the movable property of another with the intent to deprive the victim thereof, or if she unlawfully transfers immovable property of another or any interest therein with purpose to benefit herself or another not entitled thereto. [§ 223.2]
SCOPE	Common law larceny can only be of personal property.	Larceny under the MPC can be of personal or real property.
ASPORTATION	Asportation (carrying away) Required. A person is not guilty of common law larceny unless she "carries away" the personal property, however, almost any movement with the property will be deemed sufficient.	Asportation (carrying away) NOT Required.
LAND	Common law larceny does not include real property or items attached to the land (*i.e., trees*) because they are immovable, and the definition requires a "carrying away." Items that are attached to land and then severed, can be "carried away" and will fall within the scope of common law larceny, however, once detached from the land, the property is no longer considered to be part of the real property.	All property is included within the scope of MPC larceny including "immovable" property (*i.e. real property*), and "movable" property (*i.e. things growing on, or found in land*).

Offenses Against the Person

Crimes are classified into three groups: (1) crimes against habitation, (2) crimes against property, or (3) crimes against the person. While common law elements continue to be the foundation that defines these crimes, modern courts have updated many of the definitions.

	Elements	Modern Statutes
ASSAULT	An attempted battery; OR (1) intentional creation of apprehension (2) of imminent bodily injury (3) in another.	Many jurisdictions have introduced aggravated assault as a separate offense that is punishable more harshly. This can include assault with a dangerous weapon or assault with the intent to rape or murder.
BATTERY	A completed assault; OR (1) the unlawful use of force (2) against another (3) resulting in offensive touching or injury.	Many jurisdictions have introduced aggravated battery as a separate offense that is punished as a felony. This can include battery in which a deadly weapon is used, serious bodily injury is caused, or the victim is a child, woman, or police officer.
FALSE IMPRISONMENT	(1) Confinement of another (2) without legal authority or consent.	False imprisonment is largely unchanged.
KIDNAPPING	(1) Confinement and (2) movement or concealment (3) of another.	Many jurisdictions have introduced aggravated kidnapping as a separate offense. This can include kidnapping for ransom, or child stealing. Many modern statutes have done away with the movement requirement.
MANSLAUGHTER	(1) An intentional killing, (2) provoked by passion, and (3) there was no time for the actor to calm down.	In most modern courts, words alone do not constitute adequate provocation.
MURDER	(1) The unlawful killing (2) of another (3) with malice aforethought.	Modern statutes divide murder into degrees. In most states, murder is generally considered second degree murder unless it involves a deliberate and premeditated killing or felony murder, in which case it would be first degree.
RAPE	(1) Unlawful sexual intercourse (2) with a non-consenting woman, (3) by a man other than her husband, (4) by use of force, threat, or while the woman is unable to consent.	Most states now allow a husband to be convicted of raping his wife, and rape statutes are no longer limited to men as perpetrators.

Comparison Chart	The Common Law is the body of law created by judicial decisions and custom, and enforced in the absence of a relevant statute. The Model Penal Code is a scholarly text created to help state legislatures standardize the penal law to form a comprehensive and coherent body of criminal law.

Homicide

	Common Law	Model Penal Code
HOMICIDE	The killing of a human being by a human being.	A person is guilty of homicide if she unjustifiably and inexcusably takes the life of another person purposely, knowingly, recklessly or negligently. This includes murder, manslaughter and negligent homicide. [§ 210.0(1)]
MURDER	The unlawful killing of another with malice aforethought.	A killing committed purposely, knowingly, or recklessly manifesting *extreme indifference to human life*. Extreme indifference to human life is presumed if the accused killed while committing, attempted commission, or fleeing from a dangerous felony. [§ 210.2]
DEGREES OF MURDER	**First Degree Murder:** killing that is deliberate and premeditated. **Second Degree Murder:** killing with the intent to inflict grievous bodily injury, as a result of extreme recklessness ("depraved heart").	Model Penal Code makes no distinction between the degrees of murder.
FELONY MURDER	Killing another person during the commission or attempted commission, or immediate flight from an inherently dangerous felony.	It is murder if the accused killed while committing, attempting commission, or fleeing from a dangerous felony. [§ 210.2]
VOLUNTARY MANSLAUGHTER	An intentional killing brought on by adequate provocation.	A killing committed recklessly, or a killing that would otherwise be murder, but committed under the influence of extreme mental or emotion disturbance for which there is a reasonable explanation or excuse. [§ 210.3]
INVOLUNTARY MANSLAUGHTER	Death caused by criminal negligence.	Model Penal Code makes no distinction between voluntary and involuntary manslaughter.
NEGLIGENT HOMICIDE	Death caused by criminal negligence is considered involuntary manslaughter under common law.	Killings committed negligently. [§ 210.4]

Comparison Chart

The Common Law is the body of law created by judicial decisions and custom, and enforced in the absence of a relevant statute. The Model Penal Code is a scholarly text created to help state legislatures standardize the penal law to form a comprehensive and coherent body of criminal law.

Rape

	Common Law	Model Penal Code
DEFINITION	Sexual intercourse of a non-consenting woman by a man other than her husband by use of force, threat or while the woman is unable to consent.	A *male* is guilty if acting purposely, knowingly or recklessly regarding each material element of the crime, he has sex with a female: (1) that is under 10, or (2) that is unconscious, or (3) by forcing or threatening her or another person with imminent death, grievous bodily harm, extreme pain or kidnapping, or (4) drugs or intoxicates the female in a way that substantially impairs her ability to control her conduct. [§ 213.1(1)]
EXCEPTIONS	A husband cannot rape his wife.	A husband cannot rape his wife, nor can rape be committed between people "living as man and wife" even if they are not married. [§ 213.6(2)]
STATUTORY RAPE	Sexual intercourse by an adult with a person below a statutorily designated age.	**Corruption of Minors**: A *male* who has sex with a female (not his wife), or any person who engages in deviant sex or causes another to engage in deviant sex if the other person: (1) is less than 16 years old and the actor is at least 4 years older, (2) the other person is less than 21 and the actor is her guardian, or (3) the other person is in custody of the law or detained in a hospital or other institution and the actor has authority over her, or (4) the other person is a female who is induced to participate by a promise of marriage which the actor does not intend to carry out. [§ 213.3(1)]
STRICT LIABILITY	Statutory rape is a strict liability crime therefore no mens rea is needed. The actor cannot argue that he was mistaken about the minor's age or incapacity because rape depends solely on whether the act occurred with a person of a certain age.	Model Penal Code does not recognize strict liability crimes.
CORROBORATION	The testimony of the victim need not be corroborated in order to convict someone of rape.	The victim's testimony must be corroborated in order to convict for rape. [§ 213.6(5)]

Affirmative Criminal Defenses

Defenses to a crime can take the form of an ordinary defense in which the defendant argues that the prosecution is unable to prove one of the requisite elements to the crime beyond a reasonable doubt, or affirmative defenses, the burden of which is on the defendant to prove by preponderance of the evidence. Affirmative defenses are defenses which do not dispute the defendant committed the crime, but rather, attempt to prove a reasonable explanation to excuse the crime.

	Definition	Focus	Examples	
JUSTIFICATION DEFENSES	A justification defense deems conduct that is otherwise criminal to be socially acceptable and non-punishable under the circumstances.	Focus on the nature of the conduct under the circumstances.	Self-defense. Defense of another person. Defense of property.	Defense of dwelling. Necessity. Use of lawful force.
EXCULPATORY DEFENSES	An exculpatory defense acknowledges that the person has caused the harm, but asserts there is something about the individual and the circumstances that should bar punishment for the harm.	Focus on the actor, not the act, particularly on the person's moral culpability and state of mind.	Consent. Duress. Entrapment.	Insanity. Diminished Capacity. Infancy. Intoxication.
EXTRINSIC DEFENSES	Extrinsic defenses are asserted to bar conviction or prevent prosecution and are based on factors unrelated to the person's actions or state of mind.	Public Policy.	Statute of limitations. Immunity.	

Permissible Force for Justification Defenses

A justification defense deems conduct that is otherwise criminal to be socially acceptable and non-punishable under the circumstances. Justification focuses on the nature of the conduct under the circumstances.

Defense	Definition	Permissible Force	
		Non-Deadly Force	**Deadly Force**
ARREST BY A POLICE OFFICER	A person may use reasonable force in effecting a lawful arrest.	If there is probable cause to believe suspect has committed a felony; OR If the commission of crime is observed by the officer.	Only if it will prevent the escape of a felon who threatens human life.
ARREST BY A PRIVATE PERSON	A person may use reasonable force in effecting a lawful arrest.	Only if there is probable cause to believe crime was committed. Not that a reasonable or unreasonable mistake will not excuse an improper arrest.	Only to prevent the escape of a felon who actually committed the felony and threatens human life.
CRIME PREVENTION	A person may use reasonably necessary force to prevent a felony, riot or breach of the peace from taking place or from being completed.	If reasonably necessary to prevent a felony.	Only to prevent a felony in which human life is at risk.
DEFENSE OF DWELLING	A person may use non-deadly force that is no greater than reasonably necessary to prevent wrongful entry by another onto her property. In general, a person may not use deadly force to protect property, except to defend her dwelling (home) against an intruder who appears to be armed or who poses a risk to the safety of the people inside.	If reasonably necessary to prevent or stop unlawful entry.	Only if person inside the dwelling is threatened, or if it is used to prevent a dangerous felony inside the dwelling.
DEFENSE OF ANOTHER PERSON	A person may use force that is no greater than reasonably necessary to defend against an aggressor's imminent use of unlawful force.	If reasonably necessary to protect another.	Only if threatened with death or serious bodily injury.
DEFENSE OF PROPERTY	A person may use non-deadly force that is no greater than reasonably necessary to prevent the wrongful taking of her personal property.	If reasonably necessary to defend property in one's possession, except if asking to stop would suffice.	✗
NECESSITY	A person may invoke the defense of necessity if the person acted in a reasonable manner to protect the life or health of another that was being imminently threatened because there was no other reasonable choice.	If reasonably necessary to prevent greater injury.	✗
RESISTING ARREST	A person may use non-deadly force to resist an improper arrest. **Note:** There are jurisdictions that do not permit the use of force to resist improper arrest, and require the defendant to seek redress in civil court.	To prevent an improper arrest.	✗
SELF-DEFENSE	A person may use force that is no greater than reasonably necessary to defend against an aggressor's imminent use of unlawful force.	If reasonably necessary to protect oneself.	Only if threatened with death or great bodily injury.

	The Common Law is the body of law created by judicial decisions and custom, and enforced in the absence of a relevant statute. The Model Penal Code is a scholarly text created to help state legislatures standardize the penal law to form a comprehensive and coherent body of criminal law.
Comparison Chart	

Self-Defense

There is a general right to defend oneself against the use of unlawful force by another.
When successfully asserted, it is a complete defense leading to acquittal.

	Common Law	Model Penal Code
RULE	A non-aggressor is justified in using force upon another, if she reasonably believes such force is necessary to protect against imminent, unlawful force by another, so long as the force used is not excessive compared to the harm threatened.	A person is justified in using force upon another if she believes such force is immediately necessary to protect against the use of unlawful deadly force by another or the threat of rape or kidnapping. [§ 3.04(1)]
DUTY TO RETREAT	A non-aggressor need not retreat before using force in self-defense. A minority of jurisdictions require retreat if there is a safe way to do so, unless the individual is attacked in her home, or on her property.	One may <u>NOT</u> use deadly force if she can safely retreat, unless she is in her dwelling or place of work. [§ 3.04(2)(b)(ii)]
USE OF DEADLY FORCE	Deadly force used in self-protection is justified when the non-aggressor reasonably believes deadly force is necessary to repel an imminent, unlawful, and deadly attack or serious injury by the aggressor.	Deadly force is only justifiable when the person believes such force is immediately necessary to protect herself against death, serious bodily injury, kidnapping, or rape by force or threat. [§ 3.04(2)(b)]
IMPERFECT SELF-DEFENSE CLAIMS	Common law doctrine recognizing that a defendant may be entitled to a reduced punishment for an honest but unreasonable belief that the actions were necessary to counter an attack. *Note:* Under modern law, not every jurisdiction recognizes the doctrine.	An imperfect self-defense is recognized so long as it is justified by the person's subjective belief in the necessity of using the force, however, it is unavailable in a prosecution for an offense which recklessness or negligence suffices to establish culpability. [§ 3.09(2)]
RISK TO INNOCENT BYSTANDERS	A person's right to use self-defense as a justification for her actions "transfers" from the intended victim to the actual victim if she inadvertently injures someone other than the aggressor.	If a person is justified in using force against an aggressor, but uses force recklessly or negligently whereby putting an innocent bystander at risk, the use of self-defense remains available as justification for her actions towards the aggressor, but is unavailable in a prosecution for the reckless or negligent acts affecting the bystander. [§ 3.09(2)]

Comparison Chart

The Common Law is the body of law created by judicial decisions and custom, and enforced in the absence of a relevant statute. The Model Penal Code is a scholarly text created to help state legislatures standardize the penal law to form a comprehensive and coherent body of criminal law.

Defense of Property and Dwelling

	Common Law	Model Penal Code
RULE	Non-deadly force may be used to defend real or personal property from unlawful interference by another if the possessor of the property reasonably believes such force is necessary to stop imminent and unlawful seizure of the property.	An actor may use non-deadly force upon another person if the actor believes that such force is immediately necessary to prevent or terminate an entry or other trespass upon land, or to prevent the unlawful carrying away of personal property, if she believes that: (1) the other person's interference with the property is unlawful, OR (2) the intrusion upon land or taking of property deprived her (or a person by whose authority she acts) of the rightful possession of such land or property, AND (3) force is immediately necessary, OR the taker of the land or property has no claim of right to possession. [§ 3.06(1)]
DEADLY FORCE	Deadly force may never be used in defense of property unless to defend one's dwelling where the intrusion appears to pose a danger of a violent felony or the intruder is believed to be armed and dangerous to the safety of the inhabitants.	The use of deadly force is not justified unless the actor believes that the other person is: (1) attempting to take away her dwelling, AND (2) attempting to commit arson, burglary, robbery, felonious theft or property destruction and the other person used or threatened to use deadly force, OR the use of non-deadly force to prevent commission of the offense would expose the actor or another to serious bodily injury. [§ 3.06(3)(d)]
RECAPTURE OF PROPERTY	An actor may only use force to recapture her property that has been unlawfully taken if she acts promptly after it was taken.	The use of non-deadly force to re-enter land or to recapture personal property is permitted if: (1) the actor believes that she (or the person for whom she is acting) was unlawfully deprived of the property, AND (2) either the force is used immediately after the taking of the property or, if not immediate, the actor must believe that the other person has no claim of right to possession of the property. [§ 3.06(3)(c)]

Comparison Chart	The Common Law is the body of law created by judicial decisions and custom, and enforced in the absence of a relevant statute. The Model Penal Code is a scholarly text created to help state legislatures standardize the penal law to form a comprehensive and coherent body of criminal law.

Defense of Others

	Common Law	Model Penal Code
RULE	An intervenor is justified in using force against an aggressor to protect a third party to the extent that the third party would be justified in acting in self-defense.	Subject to the rules of retreat, force by an intervenor is justifiable to protect a third party when: (1) the intervenor uses no more force to protect the third-party than she would be entitled to use to protect herself based on her belief of the circumstances, AND (2) under the circumstances as the intervenor believes them to be, the third party would be justified in using such force in self-defense, AND (3) the intervenor believes that her intervention is necessary for the third party's protection. [§ 3.05(1)]
TESTS	**Alter Ego Rule:** an intervenor who comes to the aid of a third party stands in the place of the third party. To protect the third party, the intervenor is only justified in using force to the extent that the third party is justified in acting in self-defense, regardless of how the situation appears to a reasonable person.	**Subjective Rule:** the danger to the third party must seem immediate, and only the amount of force reasonably believed necessary to eliminate the risk may be exercised. [§ 3.05(1)]

Comparison Chart	The Common Law is the body of law created by judicial decisions and custom, and enforced in the absence of a relevant statute. The Model Penal Code is a scholarly text created to help state legislatures standardize the penal law to form a comprehensive and coherent body of criminal law.

Use of Force for Law Enforcement

	Common Law	Model Penal Code
NON-DEADLY FORCE FOR CRIME PREVENTION	An officer or private person is justified in using force to the extent it reasonably appears necessary to prevent a felony, riot or other serious breach of the peace.	An officer or private person is justified in using force upon another if she believes that such force is necessary to prevent another from committing suicide, inflicting serious bodily injury upon herself, or committing a crime involving or threatening bodily injury, damage to or loss of property, or a breach of the peace. [§ 3.07(5)]
DEADLY FORCE FOR CRIME PREVENTION	Deadly force is permissible for the prevention of a felony, but it may never be used to prevent a misdemeanor.	An officer or private person may not use deadly force to prevent the commission of a crime unless she believes that: (1) a substantial risk exists that the person will cause death or serious bodily injury to another unless prevented from committing the crime, AND (2) use of deadly force presents no substantial risk of injury to innocent bystanders. [§ 3.07(5)(a)(ii)(A)]
NON-DEADLY FORCE FOR EFFECTUATING AN ARREST	An officer or private person is justified in using non-deadly force to effectuate an arrest.	An officer or private person is justified in using force upon another when making or assisting in an arrest if the arresting person believes force is immediately necessary to effectuate a lawful arrest and makes known to such person the purpose of the arrest or believes the purpose of the arrest is known or cannot be reasonably made. [§ 3.07(1)-(2)]
DEADLY FORCE FOR EFFECTUATING AN ARREST	Deadly force by an <u>officer</u> is reasonable only when the person threatens death or serious bodily harm and deadly force is necessary to prevent the person's escape. A <u>private person</u> may use deadly force if reasonably necessary to arrest someone who has actually committed a felony. Mistake will not be excused by asserting that the private person had a reasonable belief.	Deadly force may be used by an <u>officer</u>, or a private person assisting someone she believes is an officer, to make an arrest for a felony if the arrestor believes that: (1) the use of deadly force creates no substantial risk of injury to innocent bystanders, AND (2) the arresting crime included the use or threatened use of deadly force or that there is a substantial risk that the arrested person will kill or seriously injure someone if the arrest is delayed. [§ 3.07(2)(b)] A <u>private citizen</u> may NOT use deadly force to make a citizen's arrest.
NON-DEADLY FORCE FOR PREVENTING ESCAPE FROM CUSTODY	An officer may use reasonable force to prevent the escape of a suspect who has already been arrested.	Force may be used to prevent a person's escape if the force could have been used to effectuate the arrest originally. [§ 3.07(3)]
DEADLY FORCE FOR PREVENTING ESCAPE FROM CUSTODY	An officer is justified to use deadly force on a suspect upon the reasonable belief that the suspect committed a felony and that such force is necessary to prevent the suspect's escape.	A guard or officer may use deadly force believed to be immediately necessary to prevent the escape of a person from prison. [§ 3.07(3)]

Exculpatory Defenses

Exculpatory defenses focus on the actor, not the act. Exculpatory defenses acknowledge the person has caused some harm, but assert that there is something about the person or circumstances that should excuse the crime.

Defense	Definition	Applicable Crimes
CONSENT	Permission by the victim to commit a crime, that was given voluntarily and not as a result of fraud or mistake, by a person who is legally capable of consenting.	Defense to crimes where lack of consent is an essential element of the crime (*i.e., rape, battery*).
DURESS	Unlawful pressure or threat exerted upon a person (usually a threat to kill or injure the person or her family) to coerce that person to perform an illegal act that she ordinarily would not perform.	Defense to ALL crimes, except homicide.
ENTRAPMENT	Unlawful pressure from a government officer or agent that induces, encourages or persuades a person to commit a crime she is not previously disposed to commit.	Defense can be applied to most crimes.
MISTAKE OF FACT	A mistake of fact is an error that is not caused by the neglect of a legal duty by the actor, but rather caused by a mistake or ignorance of a material event or circumstance.	Defense for ALL mistakes in specific intent crimes. Defense for only REASONABLE mistakes in malice or general intent crimes. NEVER a defense for strict liability crimes.
MISTAKE OF LAW	Generally, it is no defense that a person was unaware that her acts were prohibited by law or that she believed her acts were not prohibited. It is an applicable defense only if the criminal statute was not published or made reasonably available prior to the act, or the person reasonably relied on contrary statute, judicial decision or official advice or interpretation.	Defense for statutory crimes and crimes with a mental state element.
INSANITY	Exemption of a person from liability because of the existence of an abnormal mental condition, illness or defect at the time the criminal act was committed.	Defense to ALL crimes, including strict liability crimes.
INFANCY	Lack of capacity to commit a crime due to infancy can exempt a person from liability due to her physical (not mental) age if she is considered too young to be responsible for her actions at the time the criminal act was committed.	Defense to ALL crimes. Children under 7 will not be criminally liable for their actions. There is a rebuttable presumption of no liability for children under 14.
VOLUNTARY INTOXICATION	Voluntary intoxication does not excuse a person's criminal conduct, but may be used to negate the intent required for specific intent crimes.	Only a defense to specific intent crimes; NOT a defense to general intent crimes.
INVOLUNTARY INTOXICATION	Intoxication is involuntary if the actor cannot be blamed for becoming intoxicated, most likely resulting from an unexpected intoxication from a prescribed mediation, an innocent mistake as to the substance being consumed, an unexpected, temporary psychotic reaction triggered by consumption of an intoxicating substance by a person with a pre-disposing medical condition, or a coerced intoxication.	Defense to ALL crimes, including strict liability.

Comparison Chart

The Common Law is the body of law created by judicial decisions and custom, and enforced in the absence of a relevant statute. The Model Penal Code is a scholarly text created to help state legislatures standardize the penal law to form a comprehensive and coherent body of criminal law.

Duress

	Common Law	Model Penal Code
RULE	Unlawful pressure or threat exerted upon a person (usually a threat to kill or injure the person or her family) to coerce that person to perform an illegal act that she ordinarily would not perform.	Duress is a threat made by another person to use force against the accused or another unless the accused commits the offense. [§ 2.09]
ELEMENTS	(1) third party's unlawful threat; AND (2) defendant reasonably believes there is a threat of death or serious injury.	(1) The accused was compelled to commit the offense by the use or threat of immediate death or serious injury to her or another, OR (2) a person of "reasonable firmness" in the accused's situation would not have been able to resist the coercion. [§ 2.09(1)]
EXCEPTIONS	The defense is unavailable if the accused intentionally or recklessly put herself in a position that was foreseeable would result in making her a subject of duress.	The defense is unavailable if the accused recklessly put herself in the situation where she was likely to be coerced. If she negligently put herself into that position, duress is still available as a defense except for those crimes for which negligence is sufficient. [§ 2.10(2)]
APPLICABILITY	Duress is a defense to all crimes *except* murder.	Duress can be used as a defense to all crimes including murder.

Types of Insanity Defenses and Procedures

Excuses a person from liability due to an abnormal mental condition, illness or defect.

	Definition	Time of Insanity/Illness
NOT GUILTY BY REASON OF INSANITY	Exemption of a person from liability because of the existence of an abnormal mental condition, illness or defect at the time the criminal act was committed, causing the person to lack the capacity to have intended to commit the crime.	At the time the crime was committed.
INCOMPETENCY TO STAND TRIAL	The postponement of a trial until the accused regains competency.	At the time of the trial.
DIMINISHED CAPACITY	The accused may submit evidence of mental impairment to demonstrate that she lacked the requisite mental state required for the crime and the capacity to understand what she was doing or to control her actions.	At the time the crime was committed.
GUILTY BUT MENTALLY ILL	Exemption of a person from liability because although she was sane at the time of the crime and guilty of committing it, she was found to be mentally ill at the time of trial.	At the time of the trial.

Tests for Insanity

The term insanity presupposes an abnormal mental condition, illness or defect. An actor may be entitled to a verdict of "not guilty by reason of insanity" if she can demonstrate that she was insane at the time she committed the crime; however, sociopathic or psychopathic mental illness does not excuse criminal behavior.

Tests	Definition	Elements
DURHAM (PRODUCT) TEST	A person's behavior may be excused by reason of insanity if she was suffering from a mental disease or defect at the time of the offense and the criminal conduct was the product of the mental disease or defect.	(1) Person has a mental disease or defect, AND (2) crime would not have been committed *but-for* the disease or defect.
FEDERAL TEST	A person's behavior may be excused by reason of insanity if, as the result of a severe mental disease or defect at the time of the offense, she was unable to appreciate the nature and quality of her conduct or the wrongfulness of her conduct. [**18 U.S.C. § 17(a)**]	(1) Person has a mental disease or defect, AND (2) as a result of the disease or defect, the person was unable to appreciate the nature and quality of her conduct; OR as a result of the disease or defect, the person was unable to appreciate the wrongfulness of her conduct.
IRRESISTIBLE IMPULSE TEST	A person's behavior may be excused by reason of insanity if at the time of the criminal act, the person acted from an irresistible and uncontrollable impulse that rendered her unable to control her conduct.	(1) Person has a mental disease or defect, AND (2) as a result of the disease or defect, the person was unable to control her actions; OR, as a result of the disease or defect, the person was unable to conform her conduct to the laws.
M'NAGHTEN TEST	A person's behavior may be excused by reason of insanity if she suffered a mental disease causing a defect in reasoning powers and as a result, did not understand the nature and quality of the criminal act or did not know the act was wrong.	(1) A disease of the mind caused a defect of reason, AND (2) as a result of the defect, the person was unable to understand the wrongfulness of her actions; OR as a result of the defect, the person was unable to understand the nature and quality of her actions.
MODEL PENAL CODE TEST (aka AMERICAN LAW INSTITUTE TEST)	A person's behavior may be excused by reason of insanity if at the time of the criminal act, as the result of a mental disease or defect, the person lacked the substantial capacity to appreciate the criminality or wrongfulness of her conduct or to conform her conduct to the requirements of the law. [**MPC § 4.01**]	(1) Person has a mental disease or defect, AND (2) as a result of the disease or defect, the person lacked the substantial capacity to appreciate the criminality (wrongfulness) of her conduct; OR, as a result of the disease or defect, the person lacked the substantial capacity to conform her conduct to the requirements of the law.

Comparison Chart

The Common Law is the body of law created by judicial decisions and custom, and enforced in the absence of a relevant statute. The Model Penal Code is a scholarly text created to help state legislatures standardize the penal law to form a comprehensive and coherent body of criminal law.

Intoxication

	Common Law	Model Penal Code
RULE	Voluntary intoxication does not excuse a person's criminal conduct, however, involuntary intoxication can be used as a defense to the mens rea element of a crime.	Any type of intoxication can be used as a defense if it negates an element of the crime. [§2.08(1)]
RELEVANCE	Intoxication can result in an insanity, diminished capacity or mistake of fact defense.	Intoxication is only relevant if it can disprove purpose or knowledge.
TYPES OF INTOXICATION	**Voluntary Intoxication:** voluntary intoxication does not excuse a person's criminal conduct, but may be used to negate the intent necessary for a specific intent crime thereby freeing the person from criminal liability. **Involuntary Intoxication:** intoxication is involuntary if the actor cannot be blamed for becoming intoxicated most likely resulting from an unexpected intoxication from a prescribed mediation, an innocent mistake as to the substance being consumed, an unexpected temporary psychotic reaction triggered by consumption of an intoxicating substance by a person with a pre-disposing mental or physical condition or a coerced intoxication.	**Self-induced (voluntary) Intoxication:** intoxication caused by substances that the person knowingly took, which she knew or should have known have the tendency to cause intoxications, unless they were taken pursuant to medical advice or other circumstance which would be a defense to a crime. [§2.08(5)(a)] **Pathological Intoxication:** intoxication grossly excessive in degree, given the amount of the intoxicant to which the actor does not know she is susceptible. [§2.08(5)(a)] **Involuntary Intoxication:** intoxication that is not self-induced, and leads to temporary insanity. [§2.08(4)]
EXCEPTIONS	Temporary insanity based on voluntary intoxication is not a defense. Alcoholism and drug addition are both considered voluntary intoxication.	For crimes where the element of recklessness is sufficient for liability and the accused was unaware of the risk involved due to her voluntary intoxication, the unawareness does not matter because the element of recklessness does not require knowledge or intent. [§2.08(2)] Intoxication does not, in itself, constitute mental disease. [§2.08(3)]
APPLICABILITY	Voluntary intoxication is a defense to specific intent crimes. Voluntary intoxication is NOT a defense to general intent crimes.	Voluntary intoxication can be used as a defense for all crimes that were committed purposely or knowingly, but not for those committed recklessly.

Property

Acquisition of Property Rights

A property right is a protected claim of ownership over something.

	Definition	Rule	Examples
ACQUISITION BY CAPTURE	Deprivation of the natural liberty of something by killing, wounding, trapping or otherwise manifesting a state of control over it; not while trespassing on another's property.	First person to capture a resource owns such resource; property must be acquired by actual capture, mere pursuit is NOT enough. Applies to issues involving groundwater, oil, gas and wild animals.	*A hunter found a deer on vacant land and killed it even though he knew someone else was pursuing the deer. The hunter is the true owner of the deer and has superior rights to that of the person pursuing the deer because he was the first to actually kill and capture the deer.*
ACQUISITION BY DISCOVERY	Finding unknown or uncharted territory; and the symbolic taking of possession.	The first person to take possession of real or personal property is a finder. A finder's claim to personal property depends on whether the property was lost, mislaid or abandoned.	*Discovery of land in America by a European power provided absolute title.*
ACQUISITION BY CREATION	A property right is created by a person's creation of a thing. A copyright is the right to own the reproduction of the creation. A patent protects property rights in discoveries.	Creator has right to use original expression and license to any derivative use of original expression.	*A news reporting company collected news posted by a rival company, and reproduced this news as their own. Although news is common property, the articles were interpretations of the news, and products of labor of the company they were created by; therefore, the originating company has a property interest in the news it interpreted, and the other company could not misrepresent it as their own.*
ACQUISITION BY GIFT	A gift is a voluntary transfer of property from one person to another without consideration.	A valid gift must include: (1) intent, (2) constructive, symbolic or actual delivery, and (3) acceptance. Until delivery has taken place, the gift is NOT complete.	*Father wanted to give son a large painting. Father wrote son a letter expressing his intent to give son the painting. The letter is a sufficient symbolic delivery of possession to the son.*
ACQUISITION BY ADVERSE POSSESSION	Acquisition of ownership through exclusive physical possession of real property over a period of time.	Ownership by adverse possession requires exclusive, continuous, actual, open, notorious, hostile possession over a period of time.	*Neighbor builds a fence five inches over the property line of Owner. If the fence remains intact for the statutory period of time set by state law, neighbor will have a claim to the five inches of property fenced in as her own.*

Ownership Rights to Lost, Mislaid and Found Property

The first person to take possession of lost or unclaimed property with an intent to control it is called a finder. A finder's ownership rights over the property depend on: (1) location of the found item, (2) presumed intent of the true owner, and (3) the identity/status of alternative claimants of the property.

	Definition	Finder's Rights in the Property		Exceptions to Finder's Rights	Examples
		Possession	Title		
MISPLACED PROPERTY	Property intentionally placed in a certain location by the owner, and inadvertently forgotten.	✔	✘	Under common law, mislaid property goes to the owner of the property where it was found, before the finder can claim a right to such property.	*If Howard finds a mislaid wallet in the street he may keep it. However, if Howard finds a mislaid wallet next to the cash register inside a shop, he has inferior rights to the shop owner.*
LOST PROPERTY	Property unintentionally left by the owner who does not know where it is located.	✔	✘	Finder entitled to possession against all but the true owner, or prior possessors.	*Adena put her umbrella by her feet on the subway, but then forgot to pick it up before she exited. If Matt finds the umbrella, he will become the owner of the umbrella unless Adena returns to recover it.*
ABANDONED PROPERTY	Property intentionally left in a condition that makes it apparent the owner has no intention of returning to claim it.	✔	✔	None.	*Rory discarded his sofa on the sidewalk. If Adam drives by and sees the sofa, he can rightfully take possession and title to it.*

Water Rights
Individual rights to water in streams, rivers, brooks, underground watercourses and artificially constructed water channels.

Type	Definition	Applicability	Notes
RIPARIAN WATER RIGHTS*	Water does not belong to the public, it belongs to those whose land borders a watercourse (aka "riparians").	Generally used by eastern states where water is more abundant.	Riparian water use is categorized as either natural or artificial. Natural uses are those arising out of a necessity of life (*i.e., drinking or general household use*). Artificial uses are those that do not directly apply to the necessities of life (*i.e. trade, manufacturing, irrigation or profit*). Riparians can take all the water necessary for natural uses, but cannot take for artificial purposes unless there is sufficient water available for all riparians' natural use.
PRIOR APPROPRIATION WATER RIGHTS	**First in Time, First in Right:** The person who first appropriates water and puts it to reasonable and beneficial use, regardless of whether his land adjoins a watercourse, has rights superior to later appropriators.	Generally used by most water-scarce western states.	The ownership of land bordering a body of water carries with it no right to the use of the water in the absence of an appropriation. A lack of use can result in an abandonment or forfeiture of the right.

*Riparian Water Rights
Rights to water belonging to those whose land borders a watercourse.

Type	Definition	Applicability	Notes
REASONABLE USE DOCTRINE	Each person with land abutting a watercourse may take water for any reasonable use. Use should not deprive or hinder other riparians from the use and enjoyment of the water.	Used by water-rich eastern states.	Riparian owners can only enjoin use by other riparians, or recover damages for any substantial interference with needs and makes it so that the Riparian owners are not receiving enough water.
NATURAL FLOW DOCTRINE	Each riparian owner is entitled to use the natural flow of water, as long as there is no material diminution in quantity or quality.	Used in English courts during Industrial Revolution.	Domestic uses supersede commercial uses, and can be unlimited. Commercial uses are limited to reasonable uses. Riparian owners have rights to sell water, give water, use water, etc.

Water Rights to Percolating Underground Water

Percolating underground waters diffuse through the ground instead of moving in well-defined courses, and are generally extracted through wells.

Type	Definition	Applicability	Landowner's Exportation Rights
ABSOLUTE OWNERSHIP DOCTRINE	Landowners overlying underground water sources have the right to use an unlimited amount of water under their land for any purpose at any time.	Used by a minority of eastern states.	Water exportation is allowed. Landowner may freely sell or allow others to use her water.
REASONABLE USE DOCTRINE	Landowners overlying underground water sources may withdraw as much underground water as they like as long as it is not done for a malicious purpose or in a wasteful manner.	Used by about half of the states.	Water exportation is permissible so long as landowner's sale of the water does not harm other landowners who have rights to the same water.

Water Rights to Surface Water

Surface waters are those that result from rainfall or melting snow and follow no channel as they move across the surface of the land.

Type	Definition	Doctrinal Modifications and Interpretations
COMMON ENEMY DOCTRINE	Since surface water is a "common enemy" to landowners, landowners are allowed to alter drainage paths on their land (*i.e., by building dikes or modifying drainage channels*) to remove it from their property regardless of the effect on neighboring land.	Some states have modified this doctrine to hold landowners liable for unnecessary or negligent damage to neighboring land.
NATURAL FLOW DOCTRINE	Landowner may not alter natural drainage of surface water onto neighboring land, and may not modify the speed or the manner of the natural flow if it would damage neighboring land.	Since the strict application of this doctrine was inhibiting the development of land because almost every development alters the natural drainage, some states have modified this doctrine to permit reasonable changes in natural flow.
REASONABLE USE DOCTRINE	Landowner may reasonably alter the flow of surface water in good faith in order to make reasonable alterations of the land so long as the alteration does not cause unreasonable harm to neighboring land.	A balancing test is often used, weighing whether the utility of the actor's conduct reasonably outweighed the resulting gravity of harm to others.

Acquisition by Creation: Intellectual Property Protections

Intellectual property is the term given to property rights in ideas. In general, an inventor owns the object she invented, but not the design of the invention unless one of the following exceptions applies.

	Definition	Protection	Protective Period	Examples
COPYRIGHTS	The exclusive legal right given to a creator or an assignee to print, publish, perform, film, or record literary, artistic, or musical material, and to authorize others to do the same.	A copyright does not protect an idea, it protects the expression of an idea.	Copyrighted original works will be protected for the duration of the creator's life plus an additional 70 years; OR For "works made for hire," the copyright term is 95 years from the date of first publication or 120 years from the date of its creation, whichever is earliest.	*Books.* *Paintings.* *Songs.* *Articles.*
TRADEMARKS	A symbol registered with a federal agency and used to distinguish a product or associate it with a specific manufacturer.	A trademark protects a symbol that indicates the provider of particular services or goods.	The term of a federal trademark is 10 years, with 10-year renewal terms. Trademark rights can last indefinitely, as long as the owner of the trademark continues to use the trademark to identify her goods or services and timely files the request for renewal.	*Words.* *Logos.* *Symbols.* *Names.*
PATENTS	Government authority or license conferring a right or title for a set period excluding others from making, using, or selling an invention. **Design Patents** protect the decorative design, shape, configuration or appearance of an item. Design Patents are obtained when the product already exists and is being aesthetically (not functionally) modified. **Utility Patents** protect new inventions or functional modifications to existing products.	A patent protects the application of an idea.	Patent protection is applicable for 20 years from the application date; except for design patents, which last 14 years from the date the patent is granted.	*Machines.* *Processes or methods of* *Inventions.* *production.*

Gifts of Personal Property

A gift is an intentional and voluntary transfer of property without the exchange of consideration.

Type	Definition	Requirements	Revocability	Examples
GIFTS INTER VIVOS	A gift that is made during the donor's lifetime.	(1) A clear manifestation of the donor's intent to release the gift, (2) Actual delivery, AND (3) Acceptance.	✘	*Guest hands a bottle of wine to Hostess, who thanks Guest for the wine. The wine is an inter vivos gift.*
GIFTS CAUSA MORTIS	A gift that is made in expectation of the donor's impending death.	(1) A clear manifestation of the donor's intent to release the gift, (2) Donor's anticipation of immediate death, (3) Actual delivery, AND (4) Acceptance.	✔	*Alan gets shot and while on the ground bleeding says to his girlfriend, "If I don't make it, my dog Pete is yours." Alan dies. The dog is a gift causa mortis.* *A husband is sick with terminal cancer. He gives his wife his watch as an anniversary gift. This is NOT a gift causa mortis because it is not given in anticipation of death, but instead as an anniversary gift.*

Methods of Gift Delivery

To make a valid transfer of a gift, there must be intent, proper delivery, and acceptance.

	Definition	Examples
MANUAL DELIVERY	The physical transfer of possession of the gift from the donor to the donee.	*Lauren handed Matt a new baseball glove as a birthday present.*
CONSTRUCTIVE DELIVERY	Constructive delivery refers to an act amounting to a transfer of title by operation of law when actual transfer is impossible. Includes symbolic delivery.	*Kurt gives Mary the deed to his house.*
SYMBOLIC DELIVERY	The physical transfer of an object that represents the gift from the donor to the donee.	*Mike's mom gives him the keys to a new car she had purchased.*
THIRD PARTY DELIVERY	The physical transfer of a gift from an agent of the donor to the donee; the physical transfer of a gift from the donor to an agent of the donee.	*Mark buys Gayle a large painting and has the gallery deliver it to Gayle.* *Mark buys Gayle a large painting and delivers it to her home where he leaves it with her housekeeper.*

Elements of Adverse Possession

For possession to convert into title, a possessor of land needs to demonstrate the following occurred during the statutory period.

Elements	Definition	Rules	Examples
ACTUAL POSSESSION	Adverse possessor must physically use the land in the same manner that a reasonable owner would given its nature, character, and location.	The time the adverse possessor actually enters onto the land will trigger the statute of limitations to begin running.	*Living in a house on the property and paying taxes is considered actual possession.*
EXCLUSIVE POSSESSION	Adverse possessor cannot share possession with the true owner or the general public—possession must be as exclusive as would characterize an owner's normal use for such land.	People acting together and sharing only among themselves can acquire title to the property through adverse possession together as tenants in common.	*Living with the property owner in her house for the statutory period is NOT considered exclusive possession.*
OPEN AND NOTORIOUS POSSESSION	Adverse possessor's use of the land must be so visible and obvious that a reasonable owner who inspects the land will be on notice of the possessor's claim.	The adverse possessor's use of the land must be sufficiently apparent so as to serve as notice to the true owner that the adverse possessor is claiming possession over the land and to give the true owner an opportunity to defend her rights as a landowner.	*Building a house on land that belongs to another would be open and notorious possession, but living in an underground cave on that property might not be.*
ADVERSE OR HOSTILE POSSESSION	Use of the land is being made without the true owner's permission and with intent to claim the property as the possessor's own.	The state of mind of the adverse possessor is generally irrelevant. It does not matter whether the adverse possessor knows she is trespassing. Some jurisdictions require a good faith belief on the part of the possessor that they have a legal right to the property (i.e., reasonably believed the property being fenced in belonged to the possessor rather than the neighbor).	*Installing a fence that encroaches onto neighbor's property can form the basis for an adverse possession claim against the neighbor.* *Leasing a house from the owner while the owner lives abroad is **NOT** hostile possession because the owner provided the permission to use the land.*
CONTINUOUS POSSESSION	Adverse possessor's use of the land must be uninterrupted for the statutory period of time determined by the state in which the property is located.	Intermittent periods of occupancy are generally insufficient to amount to continuous use; however, incessant use is not required. Use must be no less than annual. Possessor may tack on preceding owner's time in order to satisfy the statutory time period.	*An uninvited adverse possessor living in another person's pool house each summer during the statutory period, that use is sufficient to be continuous.*

Eminent Domain and the Takings Clause

Government has the power to take title from a landowner for a legitimate public use.
Just compensation is required where a "taking" has occurred.

Type	Definition	Rule	Examples	Taking?
POSSESSORY (PER SE) TAKINGS	Permanent confiscation or physical occupation by government or by authorization of law.	Any permanent physical occupation (tangible item permanently placed upon land) by government or authorized by government constitutes a taking because it strips a landowner of her right to exclude, which is a fundamental property right.	*A local ordinance that requires landlord to permit a cable television company to install its facilities upon landlord's property is considered a taking because the ordinance takes away a landowner's fundamental right to prevent the permanent installation of a cable box upon the property.*	✔
REGULATORY TAKINGS	Government law regulating the use of land.	Although not all government regulation constitutes a taking, if the regulation denies a landowner all economic use of the land or creates a substantial diminution in the value of the land, the regulation is equivalent to a taking requiring just compensation.	*Developer purchased beachfront residential lots with the intention of building single-family homes on them. Two months later, the city enacted a law barring building of any kind on all beachfront lots. This law constitutes a taking because disallowing building of any kind denies the landowner of all substantial economic, beneficial or productive use of the land.*	✔
ZONING ORDINANCES	The regulation of the use of real property by local government, including the separation or division of a municipality into districts, the regulation of buildings in accordance with their construction or use, and the dedication of certain areas to particular uses designed to serve the general welfare.	Governments have the right to adopt zoning ordinances to regulate the permissible uses of real property without having to pay just compensation to the owner of the regulated land provided the zoning serves a legitimate interest.	*A zoning ordinance determined that a certain region of the city would be for residential use only. Even though commercial building owners in that region will now be prevented from using their property commercially, this is not a taking, but rather part of a comprehensive program to dedicate different regions to different uses.*	✘
PERMANENT MORATORIUM	A legally authorized suspension of an obligation or activity.	A permanent moratorium can be a taking if it completely thwarts investment-backed expectations for the land. Even if a permanent moratorium is subsequently overturned, compensation for the regulatory period it was in effect is due.	*After a flood destroyed part of a church's property, an act banning all building was passed. The church sued the town because it wanted to rebuild the destroyed part of its property. The act was a regulatory taking, and the church could recover damages.*	✔
TEMPORARY MORATORIUM	A legally authorized postponement of the fulfillment of an obligation or suspension of an activity.	Government regulations that are intended to be temporary from the outset do not constitute taking because they do not permanently deprive a landowner of rights in the land.	*Regional agency enacted a three year moratorium banning all building while it formulated a comprehensive land-use plan for the area. The moratorium is just a temporary regulation of property use, which does not constitute a taking.*	✘

Determining When a Government Regulation Constitutes a Taking

Local, state and federal government have the power to take title from a landowner by exercising eminent domain. However, the 5th Amendment guarantees that such private property will not be taken for public use without just compensation. Although property can be regulated without constituting a taking, if regulation is overly burdensome, it will constitute a taking.

Government Action	Rule	Examples	Taking?
LANDMARK PRESERVATION	Regulation of how a landowner may use property, where deemed necessary to promote the public interest. Landmark preservation will not constitute a taking so long as the public benefit of the regulation outweighs the private cost.	*An ordinance prohibited the modification of a landmarked building's façade. Since historical preservation is an important government interest, a city may place restrictions on the development of individual buildings as part of a comprehensive program to preserve landmarks without it being regarded as a taking.*	✘
PERMANENT PHYSICAL OCCUPATION	Any permanent physical occupation (tangible item permanently placed upon land) authorized by government constitutes a taking regardless of the public interests it may serve or the size or amount of the occupation, because it strips the landowner of the right to exclude, which is a fundamental property right.	*A local ordinance that requires a landlord to permit a cable television company to install its facilities upon the landlord's property is considered a taking because the ordinance takes away a landowner's fundamental right to prevent the permanent installation of a cable box upon the property.*	✔
CONDITIONS ON BUILDING PERMITS	When governments attach conditions to building permits, such conditions will be considered takings under circumstances in which the conditions alone would constitute a taking. Conditions are not a taking if government can prove: (1) the condition is substantially related to the state's objective, AND (2) the nature of the condition is roughly proportional to the impact of the proposed development.	*State refused to grant a landowner a permit to add an extra room to his house unless he records an easement permitting the public to cross his breach front property. This condition is a taking because there is no sufficient relationship between adding a room and the objective of providing public access.*	✔
DENIAL OF ALL VIABLE USE	When a regulation is passed depriving land of all economically beneficial use, government must compensate the owner unless it can show that the proscribed use interests were not part of his title to begin with.	*A developer purchased beachfront residential lots with the intention of building single-family homes on them. Two months later, the city enacted a law barring building of any kind on all beachfront lots. The law is a taking because disallowing building of any kind denies the owner substantially all economically beneficial or productive use of the land.*	✔
PUBLIC PURPOSE	Government can take private property, even if it is not blighted, and transfer it to private developers to achieve a legitimate public purpose. A valid public purpose can be found in a plan for economic rejuvenation of a community, even where individual properties within that community may not be blighted.	*A city had a development plan to create new jobs and increase tax and other revenue by revitalizing its waterfront and converting it into a public entertainment center. The plan sought to purchase property from willing sellers and use eminent domain to take the land from unwilling sellers. Government can take property provided it promotes a public purpose; such purpose can include promoting economic development and increasing tax revenue.*	✔
SUBSTANTIAL DIMINUTION OF VALUE THROUGH REGULATION	Where government regulation for the use of land imposes too great a hardship on the landowners, in that it makes the use of the land commercially impracticable or causes a diminution of the property value, a taking will be found and just compensation will be due to the landowners.	*A coal company sold a deed conveying only surface rights to a landowner and expressly reserving the right to remove the coal underneath. A year later, the city passes an act prohibiting the mining of coal under residential properties. While this act does not deny the land of all viable economic use, it substantially reduced the value of the coal-rich property, thereby constituting a taking.*	✔

The Process of Selling Land

Parties Enter Into Contract

Contract must be:

- in writing signed by party to be charged;
- state a definite price;
- identify definite parties; and
- identify property to be sold with sufficient specificity.

Unless expressly stated, time is not of the essence.

Implied warranty of marketability is present in every contract to sell real property unless expressly waived.

Buyer investigates seller's title to the property. If there is a defect in title, buyer must notify seller and give seller a reasonable opportunity to cure.

Under common law, the risk of loss passes to the buyer upon signing the contract, and the buyer is deemed to be the equitable owner of the land.

Closing

Seller transfers to buyer legal title to the property by delivering a deed in writing signed by seller and containing an adequate description of the land.

Transfer of real property must be done intentionally and voluntarily by seller.

When title passes, the contract is extinguished (along with the implied warranty of marketability).

The only basis for a suit by buyer after title passes is for breach of an express covenant in the deed. The six possible covenants that may appear in the deed are: seisin, right to convey, encumbrances, quiet enjoyment, warranty, or further assurances.

Recording of Title

Buyer records deed to protect her title against any subsequent bona fide purchasers.

Types of Deeds

A deed is a document used to certify ownership of a piece of land, and used to transfer ownership or other interests in the land.

Type	Definition	Covenants	Covenant Application
GENERAL WARRANTY DEED	A deed that contains six specific promises (covenants) about grantor's title to the property and warrants against any defects in the title.	Covenant of seisin. Covenant of right to convey. Covenant against encumbrances. Covenant of quiet enjoyment. Covenant of warranty. Covenant of further assurances.	Covenants warrant title against defects arising *before* and *during* the period the grantor has title.
SPECIAL WARRANTY DEED	A deed that contains six specific promises (covenants) about the grantor's title to the property, but only warrants against defects arising during the time grantor had title.	Covenant of seisin. Covenant of right to convey. Covenant against encumbrances. Covenant of quiet enjoyment. Covenant of warranty. Covenant of further assurances.	Covenants warrant title against defects arising only *during* the period the grantor has title.
QUITCLAIM DEED	A deed that makes no promises about the grantor's title to the property, but rather conveys whatever right, title or interest the grantor has in the property without making any promises regarding grantor's right to make such transfer.	None.	N/A.

Covenants of Title in Warranty Deeds

Covenants are promises from the grantor (seller) of land to the grantee (purchaser) included in the deed representing the property interest.

	Definition	Present or Future Promise?
COVENANT OF SEISIN	A promise that grantor owns the estate or interest that grantor is representing as belonging to grantor in the deed.	Present.
COVENANT OF RIGHT TO CONVEY	A promise by grantor that the person granting title has sufficient capacity and title to convey the estate which grantor by deed undertakes to convey.	Present.
COVENANT AGAINST ENCUMBRANCES	A promise that there are no easements, covenants, mortgages, liens or other encumbrances on the property or against the title or interest being conveyed, other than those specifically set forth in the deed.	Present.
COVENANT OF QUIET ENJOYMENT	A promise that the grantee will not be disturbed in her possession or enjoyment of the property by a third party's lawful assertion of superior title to the property.	Future.
COVENANT OF WARRANTY	A promise that the grantor will defend on behalf of the grantee, any reasonable claims of title by a third party and will compensate the grantee for any loss sustained by the assertion of superior title.	Future.
COVENANT OF FURTHER ASSURANCES	A promise that grantor will perform whatever acts are reasonably necessary to perfect the grantee's title if it turns out to be imperfect.	Future.

Recording Statutes

Recording statutes provide notice of interests or encumbrances affecting real property to individuals considering becoming subsequent purchasers of such property.

Type of Statute	Definition	Standard Language	Effect
NOTICE	In a jurisdiction with a notice statute, purchasers who give good value, and take property without knowledge, or record notice of a competing interest in that property will prevail.	No conveyance or mortgage of an interest in land is valid against any subsequent purchaser for value without notice thereof, unless it is recorded.	Subsequent bona fide purchaser prevails provided that purchaser neither had knowledge of a competing interest at closing, nor was there any information recorded evidencing a competing interest in that property.
RACE	In race statutes, ownership of the land between competing parties is determined solely by whichever party recorded the interest in the county recording office first. Actual or inquiry notice is irrelevant.	No conveyance or mortgage of an interest in land is valid against any subsequent purchaser whose conveyance is first recorded.	Grantee who records first prevails.
RACE-NOTICE	In race-notice statutes, in order for subsequent purchasers who give good value to take ownership interests that are superior to competing interests, such subsequent purchase must be without knowledge or record notice of the competing interest, AND that subsequent purchaser must record their interest first, before the competing interest.	No conveyance or mortgage of an interest in land is valid against any subsequent purchaser for value without notice thereof whose conveyance is first recorded.	Subsequent bona fide purchaser prevails only if that purchaser takes the property without knowledge of a competing interest AND records first.

Types of Tenancies

Temporary rights of possession in real property.

Type	Definition	Notice Required for Termination	Examples
TENANCY FOR YEARS	Tenancy for a fixed period whose expiration date is predetermined.	No notice is required since the parties know exactly when the term of years will end.	*To A "from January 1, 2013 to December 31, 2015."*
PERIODIC TENANCY	Tenancy that continues for successive intervals until proper notice of termination is given by landlord or the tenant.	Notice must be given before a period at least equal to the length of the lease period, except for tenancies of one year or greater, in which case only six months notice is required. The notice requirement may be modified by agreement.	*To A "from month to month" (one month notice is required).* *To A "from year to year" (only six months notice is required).*
TENANCY AT WILL	Tenancy for no fixed durational period.	A tenancy may be terminated by either party at any time without notice, but a reasonable time to vacate must be provided.	*To A "for as long as she wants to live here."*
TENANCY AT SUFFERANCE	Tenancy is created when the tenant who was rightfully in possession has remained past the lease expiration date.	No notice required, lease already terminated. Landlord's remedies include eviction or creation of a periodic tenancy.	*To A "until December 31, 2013."* *If A remains in possession on January 1, 2014, landlord has the option to evict A, or hold her to another term equal in length to the term of the original lease.*

Concurrent Estates

Right to ownership or possession in property between two or more individuals.

	Definition	Creation	Right to Sell or Transfer	Termination	Right of Survivorship	Examples
JOINT TENANCY WITH RIGHT OF SURVIVORSHIP	Simultaneous ownership of property by two or more people with a right of survivorship. Each person owns a single, undivided interest in the property. Unity in possession, interest, time and title.	Creation of a joint tenancy is not presumed. Document must state "joint tenants with right of survivorship." Without this language, it a tenancy in common is presumed.	A joint tenant can sell or transfer her interest at any time for any reason during the tenant's lifetime, but not after death.	Agreement of joint tenants. Forced sale. Conveyance by one joint tenant. Murder of one co-tenant by another. Simultaneous deaths of co-tenants. Voluntary or involuntary partition.	✔	*"To A and B as joint tenants with the right of survivorship."*
TENANCY BY THE ENTIRETY	Tenancy by the entirety is a joint tenancy with right of survivorship between a husband and wife.	Parties must be husband and wife at the time the deed is executed.	Neither party can independently transfer his or her share without the other.	Divorce. Death (property goes to surviving spouse). Execution by joint creditor. Mutual agreement. Voluntary partition.	✔	*"To husband and wife as tenants by entirety."*
TENANCY IN COMMON	Simultaneous ownership of property by two or more people with no right of survivorship. Each person owns a separate, not necessarily equal share, and each has a right to possess the whole.	It is presumed if co-tenants are not husband and wife or if the words "with a right of survivorship" are not stated on the deed.	Any co-tenant can sell or transfer her interest at any time during or after their lifetime for any reason.	Either tenant can transfer their interest to a third party. Agreement of the parties. Forced sale. Voluntary or involuntary partition.	✘	*"To A and B."* *"To A and B as tenants in common."*

Landlord's Duties, Tenant's Rights and Remedies

Landlord has certain duties that are owed to tenant in exchange for the payment of rent. Some of these duties are explicit in the lease, some are implied and some are required by law. If landlord breaches any of his obligations, tenant has certain remedies that she can seek.

Landlord's Duty	Definition	Landlord's Breach	Tenant's Rights and Remedies
SELECTION OF TENANTS	Landlord is free to choose who she would like her tenants to be, however, landlord may not discriminate when selecting tenants.	Landlord is in breach of the Fair Housing Act is she refuses to rent to a tenant based upon the tenant's race, ethnicity, gender, religion, handicap, familial status or national origin.	Monetary damages.
DUTY TO DELIVER POSSESSION	Most states require landlord to deliver actual possession of the premises to tenant at the beginning of the lease term.	Landlord is in breach if she fails to remove all prior tenants from the property prior to the start of a new lease.	Monetary damages.
COVENANT OF QUIET ENJOYMENT	Even if not explicit in the lease, landlord is deemed to have covenanted that during the lease term, no one will interfere with tenant's use and enjoyment of the premises.	**Actual Eviction:** tenant is physically evicted from the entire leased premises.	Tenant's obligation to pay rent terminates.
		Partial Actual Eviction: tenant is evicted from a substantial portion of the leased premises.	Tenant's obligation to pay rent is abated entirely until possession is restored.
		Constructive Eviction: act or omission by landlord which substantially interferes with tenant's use and enjoyment of the leased premises by rendering the premises substantially unsuitable for the purpose for which it was leased.	Tenant may terminate lease and seek monetary damages.
WARRANTY OF HABITABILITY	Even if not explicit in the lease, landlord is deemed to have warranted that landlord will deliver and maintain the premises in a condition reasonably suitable for human habitation.	Landlord is in breach is she fails to fix any substantial defect that affects the health and/or safety of the tenant.	Tenant may withhold rent, paying an amount equal to the fair market value of the defective property. Tenant may repair the defects and deduct the cost from rent owed to landlord. Tenant may remain in possession, pay rent and seek monetary damages. Tenant may terminate lease and seek monetary damages.

Tenant's Duties, Landlord's Rights and Remedies

Tenant's Duty	Definition	Breach	Landlord's Remedy
PAYMENT OF RENT	Tenant is obligated to timely pay the agreed upon rent to landlord.	Regardless of whether tenant remains on the premises or abandons it, tenant will be in beach of her duty to pay rent if she fails to timely pay the rent in the manner agreed upon in the lease.	Evict tenant, and/or Sue tenant for lost rent.
TO REPAIR	Tenant has a duty to repair any damage caused by her or her invitees. Tenant may have to make small repairs in order to return the leased premises in substantially the same condition as at the commencement of the lease term, absent ordinary wear and tear. Tenant is not obligated to make extensive repairs.	Tenant is in breach if she fails to repair damages that she intentionally or negligently made to the premises. Tenant is in breach if she makes significant alterations to the premises, even if the alterations increase the value of the premises, unless the alterations were reasonably necessary for the tenant to use the leased premises in a manner that is reasonable under the circumstances.	Monetary damages.
NOT TO MAKE ILLEGAL USE OF THE PREMISES	Tenant is prohibited from using the leased premises for illegal purposes.	Tenant does not breach her duty by engaging in occasional unlawful conduct, such as infrequent use of marijuana. Tenant is in breach of her duty if she uses the premises illegally in a way that is continuous and habitual, such as prostitution or gambling. Tenant does not breach her duty if she engages in illegal activity outside of the premises.	Continuous or habitual illegal use of premises allows a landlord to terminate the lease, evict tenant and recover monetary damages.

Fixtures

Determination of whether an item is chattel or a fixture depends on whether the item is affixed to real property. Affixation is the act of attaching an item of personal property to real property. If an item is affixed to real property it is a fixture, if not, it is chattel.

		Definition	Type of Lease	Type of Property	Ownership	Removal Rights	Examples
	CHATTEL	Goods or other moveable, tangible items.	Residential or Commercial.	Personal property.	Tenant retains ownership.	Tenant may remove chattel at the end of the lease term.	*Tenant brings a coffee maker when she moves in. Even though she may plug it in, the coffee maker remains tenant's chattel.*
FIXTURES	**ORDINARY FIXTURES**	Chattel that becomes real property when affixed in a permanent manner to real estate.	Residential.	Real property.	After installation, fixture becomes part of the real property owned by landlord.	Tenant may NOT remove fixture at the end of the lease term.	*Tenant has lumber delivered. At the time of the delivery, lumber is chattel; however, if tenant uses the lumber to build a deck attached to the house, the lumber will be considered a fixture and will stay with the house when tenant's lease expires.*
	TRADE FIXTURES	A piece of equipment attached to the real estate, which is used in a trade or business.	Commercial.	Personal property.	Tenant retains ownership.	Tenant may remove trade fixture at the end of the lease term, however, tenant must repair any damage caused by the removal or compensate landlord for any damage. If the fixture remains after expiration of the lease term, it becomes property of the landlord.	*A dentist's chair is a trade fixture if it is being used as part of a dentist's business. Although it is attached to the property, the dentist may take the chair with her when she moves to a different location.*

Transfer Rights Under a Lease

Absent an express restriction within a lease to the contrary, landlords and tenants have the right to assign or sublet their leasehold interests.

	Definition	Consent Required	Liability for Lease Covenants	Transferor's Rights	Privity of Contract	Privity of Estate	Examples
ASSIGNMENT BY TENANT	Once a lease is assigned from the original tenant to a new tenant, the new tenant and the landlord are in privity of contract; each is responsible to the other for the covenants in the original lease. Original tenant remains secondarily liable.	No, unless expressly required under the lease.	New tenant is liable to landlord on all covenants that run with the land. Original tenant remains secondarily liable for rent and *all* other covenants in the lease.	Transfer of the tenant's entire interest in the estate.	✘	✔	*Landlord leases an apartment to tenant and tenant promises to pay $900 a month rent. Tenant then assigns the lease to a new tenant. If landlord is not paid the following month, landlord can sue both the new tenant and the original tenant.*
ASSIGNMENT BY LANDLORD	Once a lease is assigned to a new landlord, the new landlord and the tenant become responsible to each other for all of the covenants in the original lease that run with the land. Original landlord remains secondarily liable.	Tenant's consent is *not* required.	New landlord is liable to tenant on all covenants that run with the land. Original landlord remains liable on *all* covenants in the lease.	Transfer of the landlord's entire interest in the estate.	✔	✘	*Landlord leases an apartment to tenant for a year, then sells the building and assigns the lease to a new landlord who fails to provide heat to tenant in the winter. Tenant can sue the new landlord and the original landlord to enforce her rights under the lease.*
SUBLEASE	Once a lease between a landlord and a tenant is created, tenant can enter into a subsequent sublease with a new tenant (subtenant) for the same property being leased unless the lease agreement expressly restricts the tenant's ability to sublease the premises.	No, unless expressly required under the lease.	Neither subtenant nor landlord are personally liable to one another on any covenants in the original lease, and neither can enforce the covenants under the lease. It is the original tenant who remains liable to the landlord for rent, and it is the original tenant only who can enforce the landlord's covenants.	Tenant retains rights or interest under the original lease.	✘	✘	*Landlord leases an apartment to tenant and tenant promises to pay $900 a month rent. Tenant then subleases the apartment to a subtenant. If landlord is not paid the rent, landlord cannot sue the subtenant for monies owed, she can only pursue damages from the original tenant.*

A Summary of Servitudes

Certain types of land interests exist between parties that do not involve the transfer of ownership, but rather the right to use or restrict the use of someone else's land.

	Type	Definition	Creation	Examples	Remedy
EASEMENTS	Affirmative Easements	An affirmative easement is the right to use another's property for a specific purpose.	Grant. Prescription. Implication. Necessity. Estoppel.	*Omar grants Julia right of way across Omar's property; Julia has an affirmative easement.*	Injunction or monetary damages.
	Negative Easements	A negative easement is the right to prevent another from performing an otherwise lawful activity on their property.	Writing signed by grantor. No negative easement arises by implication or by operation of law.	*A negative easement might restrict a landowner's ability to build beyond a designated height, so as to preserve the neighbor's view.*	Injunction or monetary damages.
SERVITUDES	REAL COVENANTS	A real covenant is a written promise to do or not do something on the land. These promise runs with the land (not the owners), and future landowners may enforce or be burdened by the restrictions agreed to by their predecessors. Note that all covenants can be enforced as equitable servitudes.	Writing signed by Grantor.	*When Adam buys Laurie's land he sees in the deed that he cannot put a chemical plant on the land. This promise had been made between Laurie and her neighbor to make sure the neighbor's soil stayed clean for his crops. If Adam decides to build a chemical plant, he will be in breach of the covenant and can be sued by the neighbor.*	Monetary damages. A party desiring an injunction would need to sue for violation of an equitable servitude rather than a covenant.
	Equitable Servitudes	Equitable servitudes are promises concerning the use of land that benefit and burden the original parties to the promise and their successors. Note that not all equitable servitudes can be enforced as covenants.	Writing signed by grantor or by implication from a common plan, scheme or development.	*Al's land is part of a residential subdivision. Al's deed says nothing about the land being limited to residential use. Jim purchases Al's land and decides the location is perfect for a slaughterhouse. A neighbor whose home is part of the same subdivision can seek an injunction to prevent Jim from operating a slaughterhouse, but will be unable to seek monetary damages.*	Injunction.
	Reciprocal Negative Servitudes	Where individual lots within a subdivision or common plan or scheme contain an express restriction within their deeds, said restrictions will be implied to be contained in all deeds within that subdivision or common plan, scheme or development. Such implied restrictions are reciprocal negative servitudes.	Implication.	*A developer subdivides land into 50 lots. She conveys the first 46 by deeds expressly containing covenants accepted by the respective grantees, that the lots will only be used for residential purposes. Although the deed to the 47th lot contains no express residential restriction, a reciprocal negative servitude exists because there was a common scheme evidenced by the covenants in the first 46 deeds and any purchaser of lot 47 is on inquiry notice of the negative covenant because of the uniform residential character of the other lots.*	Injunction.

Creation and Termination of Rights in the Land of Another

Certain types of land interests exist between parties that do not involve the transfer of ownership, but rather the right to use the other's land. These rights can be created and terminated in a variety of ways.

	Definition	Methods of Creation	Methods of Termination	
EASEMENTS	A non-possessory right to enter and use another's land for a limited purpose.	Grant. Prescription. Implication from prior use. Necessity. Estoppel.	Termination of a stated condition of termination. Merging of ownership of the benefitted and burdened land. Execution of a written release from the benefit holder. Permanent physical abandonment by the owner of the privilege with demonstrated intent to relinquish right.	Estoppel. Prescription. End of necessity for easement. Condemnation or destruction of burdened property. Sale to a bona fide purchaser without notice of an easement by grant.
PROFITS	A non-possessory right to enter another's land to remove natural resources.	Grant. Prescription. Implication from prior use. Estoppel. CANNOT be created by necessity.	Termination of a stated condition of termination. Merging of ownership of the benefitted and burdened land. Execution of a written release from the benefit holder. Permanent physical abandonment by the owner of the privilege.	Estoppel. Prescription. Condemnation or destruction of burdened property. Misuse of profit by unduly increasing the burden.
REAL COVENANTS	Real covenants are written promises between landowners, to do or not to do something on the other's land. These promises run with the land (not the owners), and future landowners may enforce or be burdened by the promises made by their predecessors. Covenants can be enforced as covenants and/or equitable servitudes depending upon the remedy sought.	Execution of a writing signed by grantor.	Merging of ownership of the benefitted and burdened land. Execution of a written release from the benefit holder. Condemnation of the burdened property.	Abandonment. Estoppel. Sale to a bona fide purchaser without notice.
EQUITABLE SERVITUDES	A promise concerning the use of land that benefits and burdens the original parties to the promise and their successors. Not all equitable servitudes can be enforced as covenants.	Execution of a writing signed by grantor. Implication from common scheme of development of a residential subdivision.	Merging of ownership of the benefitted and burdened land. Execution of a written release from the benefit holder. Estoppel.	Abandonment. Condemnation of the burdened property. Sale to a bona fide purchaser without notice.

Creation of Easements

An easement is a non-possessory right to enter and use another's land for a limited purpose.

	Creation	Writing Requirement
EXPRESS EASEMENTS	An easement granted in a deed or other writing that identifies the parties, states an intent to create an easement, describes the land, and is signed by the grantor.	✔
EASEMENTS IMPLIED FROM PRIOR EXISTING USE	An easement may be implied if, prior to the time a larger tract of land was divided, a use existed on one part that benefitted the other, and that use remains necessary to the dominant part, is open and apparent, and has remained in continuous use since the division.	✘
EASEMENTS IMPLIED BY NECESSITY	An easement by necessity is implied when a tract of land is divided, and by its division, one part is deprived of access to a public road or has been otherwise rendered useless or unproductive. Primarily used under circumstances in which property is landlocked.	✘
PRESCRIPTIVE EASEMENTS	An easement by prescription is created if use of another's land has been continuous and uninterrupted, open without an attempt to conceal, and without the owner's permission throughout the requisite statutory period.	✘
EASEMENTS BY ESTOPPEL	A license is oral permission to go onto another's land. Licenses are generally revocable, but if a license is entered into in good faith, and in reliance on the promise of another that the use will be permitted, the license will become irrevocable, and an easement by estoppel is created.	✔

Requirements for Covenants to Run with the Land

A real covenant is a written promise to do or not do something on land. The promise remains with the land, and future landowners may enforce or be burdened by the promise made by their predecessors.

Requirements	Definition	Needed for <u>Burden</u> to Stay with the Land	Needed for <u>Benefit</u> to Stay with the Land
INTENT	The parties entering into the covenant must have intended for the future landowners to enforce the covenant. Parties' intentions are usually written in the deed to the land or the contract.	✔	✔
NOTICE	Future landowners must have notice of the covenant to be bound by it. Notice is given when the covenant is recorded, but if it fails to get recorded, future landowners burdened by the covenant will take the land free of the restriction.	✔	✘
HORIZONTAL PRIVITY	There must have been some relationship between the parties who originally entered into the covenant, in which they shared some interest in the land burdened by the covenant.	✔	✘
VERTICAL PRIVITY	Vertical privity concerns the relationship between an original covenanting party and its successors. Vertical privity exists only if a successor takes the entire estate in land previously held by the original covenanting party.	✔	✔
TOUCH AND CONCERN	The effect of the covenant is to make the land more useful or valuable to the covenanting parties, or to somehow benefit the land. The covenant must affect the parties as landowners rather than as individuals.	✔	✔
WRITING	All covenants must be in writing pursuant to the Statute of Frauds. Covenants are usually written in the deed to the land or the contract.	✔	✔

Future Rights in the Land of Another

Certain types of land interests exist between parties that involve the right to use or restrict the use of someone else's land. Upon the transfer of ownership of the land, some of these rights will exist between the future landowners and some will not.

	Definition	Type	Future Rights	Examples
EASEMENTS	A non-possessory right to enter and use another's land for a limited purpose.	**Easement Appurtenant:** An easement that benefits the landowner in the use of another's tract of land.	The benefit and burden of an easement appurtenant automatically passes with transfers of the land, regardless of whether it is mentioned in the conveyance.	*Alana owns Whiteacre, located between Blackacre and a public road. Alana grants anyone who owns Blackacre a right to cross Whiteacre to reach the road. If Blackacre is sold to Hallie, Hallie will continue to have a right to cross Whiteacre.*
		Easement in Gross: An easement that benefits only the specified individual the use of another's tract of land.	An easement in gross is generally not transferrable; however, modern courts have recognized a limited right to transfer easements in gross to third parties where the easement is for a commercial purpose.	*Harper grants neighboring landowner Max the right to post a billboard on her property. If Harper sells her property, the burden of the easement will automatically pass with ownership of the property. In contrast, if Max sells his property, the right to post the billboard will not automatically transfer.*
PROFITS	A non-possessory right to enter another's land to take natural resources. Absent an express indication to the contrary, profits are presumed to be "in gross."	**Profit Appurtenant:** May *only* be used by the owner of the adjacent property. A properly recorded profit will remain even if the ownership of the land upon which the profit exists changes hands.	A profit appurtenant follows the ownership of the dominant estate.	*Ash's property has very fertile soil because it borders a stream. Since Ash's neighbor Caleb's soil is inland and very dry, Ash allows Caleb to take some of her soil so that Caleb can grow crops on his land. When Ash sells her property, Caleb will no longer have a profit in the soil.*
		Profit in Gross: Freely assignable or otherwise transferrable by its owner, unless expressly identified as being exclusive to the grantee.	A profit in gross belongs to the individual holder, and is assignable or transferrable.	*Bob grants all town residents the right to fish in his pond. A town resident can transfer her right to fish in Bob's pond to a friend in another town, unless the profit expressly prohibits such transfer.*
REAL COVENANTS	A written promise that runs with the land, to do or not do something on the land.		The <u>burden</u> will stay or "run" with land if: (1) it is intended to by its makers, (2) it is in writing, (3) notice is given to successors, (4) it touches and concerns the land, AND (5) there is horizontal and vertical privity. The <u>benefit</u> will stay or "run" with land if: (1) it is intended to by its makers, (2) it is in writing, (3) it touches and concerns the land, AND (4) there is vertical privity.	*When Adam buys Laurie's land he sees in the deed that he cannot put a chemical plant on the land. This promise had been made between Laurie and her neighbor to make sure the neighbor's soil stayed clean for his crops. If Adam decides to build a chemical plant, he will be in breach of the covenant and can be sued by the neighbor.*

Future Rights in the Land of Another, *continued*

	Definition	Future Rights	Examples
EQUITABLE SERVITUDE	A promise concerning the use of land that benefits and burdens the original parties to the promise and their successors.	The <u>burden</u> will stay with land if: (1) it is intended to by its makers, (2) it is in writing or implied from a common plan, (3) notice is given to the successors, AND (4) it touches and concerns the land. The <u>benefit</u> will stay with land if: (1) it is intended to by its makers, (2) it is in writing or implied from a common plan, AND (3) it touches and concerns the land.	*Mo's land is part of a residential subdivision. Mo's deed says nothing about the land being limited to residential use. Pete purchases Mo's land and decides to open a restaurant. A neighbor whose home is part of the same subdivision can seek an injunction to prevent Pete from opening a restaurant, but will be unable to seek monetary damages.*

Requirements for Equitable Servitudes to Run with the Land

Equitable servitudes are promises concerning the use of land that benefit and burden the original parties to the promise and their successors.

Requirements	Definition	Needed for <u>Burden</u> to Stay with the Land	Needed for <u>Benefit</u> to Stay with the Land
INTENT	The parties creating the servitude must have intended for successors to enforce the servitude. Parties' intentions do not need to be written, they can be inferred from the purpose of the servitude and the circumstances upon which it was created.	✔	✔
NOTICE	Successors in interest must have notice of the servitude to be bound by it. Notice is sufficient if the servitude is recorded or it can be implied from the common scheme of development of a residential subdivision.	✔	✘
TOUCH AND CONCERN	The effect of the servitude is to make the land more useful or valuable, or to somehow benefit the land. The servitude must affect the parties as landowners, rather than simply as individuals.	✔	✔
PRIVITY	Privity concerns the relationship between the parties who originally entered into the servitude and their successors in interest. **NO PRIVITY NEEDED!** Because courts do not enforce servitudes as a personal interests in law entitling a party seeking enforcement to monetary damages, but rather as an equitable property interest with an injunction being the only available remedy, privity is not required.	✘	✘
WRITING OR IMPLIED FROM COMMON PLAN	All equitable servitudes must be created by a writing, unless it is a negative equitable servitude that may be implied from a common scheme for the development of a residential subdivision, so long as landowners have notice of the agreement.	✔	✔

The Rule Against Perpetuities

The Rule Against Perpetuities (RAP) is a legal prohibition against indefinitely restraining property from being transferred in that it forbids future interests that could potentially vest after the established period. The rule provides that the maximum period during which the transfer of title to real property may be restricted is a "life in being plus 21 years." The rule was created to limit any individual's power to control ownership of real property after death and to ensure the transferability of real property.

RULE	No property interest is good unless it must vest, if at all, not later than 21 years after the death of some life in being at the creation of the interest.
RAP APPLIES TO	Contingent Remainders. / Executory Interests. / Vested Remainders Subject to Open. // Powers of Appointment. / Rights of First Refusal. / Options to Purchase.
LANGUAGE BREAKDOWN	**"Must vest"** An interest becomes "vested" when: (1) it becomes a present possessory estate, OR (2) it comes an indefeasibly vested remainder or a vested remainder subject to total divestment. **"Lives in being"** The remaining duration of the life of a person who is in existence at the time the perpetuities period begins. **"If at all"** The interest does not need to vest within the perpetuities period in order to be valid.
WHEN PERPETUITIES PERIOD BEGINS	The perpetuities period in the case of a <u>will</u> begins to run on the date of the testator's death. The perpetuities period in the case of a <u>revocable trust</u> begins to run on the date the trust becomes irrevocable. The perpetuities period in the case of an <u>irrevocable trust</u> begins to run on the date the trust is created. The perpetuities period in the case of a <u>deed</u> or an intervivos transfer begins to run on the date of delivery.
EXCEPTIONS	**Charity-to-Charity Exception.** Gifts from one charity to another are not subject to the rule against perpetuities. The rule against perpetuities does not apply to future interests that revert to the grantor: reversion, possibility of reverter, right of entry.

Rule Against Restraints on Alienation

As a matter of public policy, courts will invalidate restrictions placed on the alienation of real property. This rule was created to ensure the transferability of property.

LANGUAGE OF THE RULE	Prohibition of the transferability of a legal interest in real property is void.
TYPES OF RESTRAINTS ON ALIENATION	**Forfeiture Restraints.** A grant under which any attempted transfers made by grantee forfeits the grantee's interest (*i.e. O conveys land "to A, but if A ever attempts to sell the land, then to B"*). **Disabling Restraints.** A grant under which attempted transfers by grantee are ineffective (*i.e. O conveys land "to A, but any transfer of interest in the land shall be null and void"*). Such restraints are *always* void. **Promissory Restraints.** A grant under which an attempted transfer breaches a covenant (*i.e. O conveys land "to A, so long as A promises that the land will never be transferred by any means"*).
EFFECT OF RULE	The type of estate conveyed influences the application of the rule.
VALID RESTRAINTS ON ALIENATION	Forfeiture and promissory restraints *can be valid* on life estates. Forfeiture restraints on transferability *can be valid* on future interests. Reasonable restrictions in commercial transactions. Rights of first refusal. Restrictions on assignment and sublease of leaseholds.
INVALID RESTRAINTS ON ALIENATION	Complete restraints on fee simple estates. All disabling restraint on legal interests.

Freehold Estates

A freehold estate is the exclusive right to the use and possession of real property for an indefinite period.

	Estate	Language	Duration	Transferability	Future Interest	Future Interest Holder
	FEE SIMPLE ABSOLUTE	*To A.* *To A and her heirs.*	Absolute ownership, of potentially infinite duration.	Alienable. Devisable. Descendible.	None.	None.
	FEE TAIL	*To A, and the heirs of her body.*	Lasts only as long as there are lineal blood descendants of grantee. Note that most states do not recognize the fee tail, and treat the interest as a fee simple absolute.	Passes automatically to grantee's lineal descendants.	Reversion or Remainder.	Reversion (Grantor). Remainder (3rd Party).
DEFEASIBLE FEES	**FEE SIMPLE DETERMINABLE**	*To A while …* *To A until …* *To A so long as …*	Potentially infinite, so long as event does not occur.	Alienable. Devisable. Descendible. Subject to condition.	Possibility of Reverter.	Grantor.
	FEE SIMPLE SUBJECT TO A CONDITION SUBSEQUENT	*To A, but if X event happens, grantor reserves the right to re-enter.* *To A, provide that …* *To A, on condition that …* *To A, but if …*	Potentially infinite, so long as the condition is not breached and, thereafter until the holder of the right of entry timely exercises the power of termination.	Alienable. Devisable. Descendible. Subject to condition.	Right of Entry.	Grantor.
	FEE SIMPLE SUBJECT TO AN EXECUTORY LIMITATION	*To A, but if X happens, then to B.*	Forever, so long as stated contingency does not occur.	Alienable. Devisable. Descendible. Subject to condition.	Executory Interest.	Third Party.
	LIFE ESTATE	*To A for life.* *To A for the life of B.*	Measured by life of transferee or by some other measuring life.	Alienable. Devisable. Descendible if *pur autre vie* and measuring life is alive.	Reversion or Remainder.	Reversion (Grantor). Remainder (3rd Party).

Future Interests: Remainders

Future interests are non-possessory rights that are capable of becoming possessory in the future. A remainder is a future interest that takes effect upon the expiration of the preceding property interest.

	Type	Definition	Examples	Reverts to Grantor
VESTED REMAINDERS	**INDEFEASIBLY VESTED**	It is certain of becoming possessory and cannot be divested.	*O to A for life, then to B and his heirs.*	✘
	SUBJECT TO DIVESTMENT	A future event that may cause an individual with an otherwise vested remainder to lose that property interest.	*O to A for life, then to B and his heirs, but if B uses land for commercial purposes, then to C. B has a vested remainder, subject to divestment.*	✘
	VESTED REMAINDER SUBJECT TO OPEN	Vested remainder which may need to be shared with additional owners in the future because the group or class to whom the interests was transferred remains open to the possibility of additional member (i.e. "to A's grandchildren").	*To A for life, then to A's children and their heirs. To date, A has one child, B, but could have additional children in the future. B has a vested remainder subject to open.*	✘
CONTINGENT REMAINDERS	**CONDITION PRECEDENT**	A property interest to take effect provided that an uncertain event occurs, and which may never take effect.	*O grants Blackacre to A for life, then to B if B survives A.*	✔
	GRANTEE UNBORN OR UNASCERTAINABLE	A property which cannot immediately vest because the beneficiary is subject to a condition precedent which would identify said beneficiary, and which has not yet occurred.	*To A for life, then to A's eldest son and his heirs.* *A is presently childless.*	✔

Future Interests Held by Grantor

Future interests are non-possessory rights that are capable of becoming possessory in the future.

	Definition	Method of Reversion	Occurrence	Examples	Automatic?
REVERSION	Any future interest retained by the grantor who transfers property to another. A reversion occurs when a property owner makes an effective transfer of property to another but retains some future right to the property. A reversion differs from a remainder because a reversion arises by operation of law rather than by an act of the parties, and belongs to the grantor rather than a third party.	Reverts to grantor upon the termination of an interest.	Follows a life estate or any other terminable interest.	*O grants Blackacre to A for life.* *If A dies, Blackacre automatically is returned to O.*	✔
POSSIBILITY OF REVERTER	A contingent future interest in real property that a grantor of a determinable fee possesses after she has conveyed property.	Reverts to grantor upon the occurrence of the stated event.	Almost always follows a fee simple determinable, but it can follow a life estate.	*O grants Blackacre to A, for as long as A refrains from smoking cigarettes.* *If A begins smoking, the property transfers back to O.*	✔
RIGHT OF ENTRY	When an owner transfers an estate subject to a condition subsequent and retains the power to cut short or terminate the estate, the grantor has what is called a right of entry. Right of entry is distinguishable from reversion in that it requires an affirmative act by the grantor rather than arising automatically by operation of law as in the case of a reversion.	Reverts to grantor when grantor exercises her right of entry.	Follows a condition subsequent.	*O grants Blackacre to A, on condition that A refrains from playing loud music; O retains the right to terminate the interest upon A's failure to comply with the stated condition.* *In order for the property to return to O, O will need to make an affirmative effort to exercise the right of entry.*	✘

Future Interests Held by Grantee

Future interests are non-possessory rights that are capable of becoming possessory in the future.

	Definition	Timing	Occurrence	Examples
REMAINDER	A future interest created in the grantee that may become a present, possessory estate upon the natural termination of a prior estate created by the same instrument.	At any time *after* the present possessory estate ends.	Can only follow a fee tail, life estate or term of years. Cannot follow a fee simple interest.	*O conveys property to A for life, then upon A's death, to B.* B has a remainder because B will not be entitled to possession of the property until A dies. Upon A's death, B will be entitled to present possession of the property.
EXECUTORY INTEREST	A future interest created in a grantee that divests or "cuts short" another estate or interest, to become possessory.	At any time *during* the present possessory estate.	Any interest that follows a fee and is held by a third person.	*To O until such time when A has children, then to A.* O's interest will automatically divest to A if and when she has children. Since that can happen at any time during O's ownership of the property, A has an executory interest. Upon A having children, A will be entitled to present possession of O's property.

Executory Interests

Future interests are non-possessory rights that are capable of becoming possessory in the future. An executory interest is a future interest created in the grantee that divests or "cuts short" another estate or interest to become possessory.

	Definition	Whose Estate It Divests	Timing	Examples
SHIFTING EXECUTORY INTEREST	A future interest in a grantee that divests a preceding estate of someone other than the grantor. Shifting executory interests may be premised on any event, irrespective of whether that event is under the control of one party or the other, or if it is an external event under the control of neither party.	Someone other than the Grantor.	Divests prior to its natural termination.	*To A, but if B returns home, then to B.* B has a shifting executory interest.
SPRINGING EXECUTORY INTEREST	A springing executory interest divests of cuts short the grantor's own interest, in favor of the grantee.	Grantor.	Follows a lapse in possession. OR Divests after it was granted estate, but usually before its natural termination.	*To A and her heirs if A graduates from law school.* A has a springing executory interest.

Alienation and Division of Possessory Estate

A present interest is an interest that is current and possessory. Below is a demonstration of the ways in which grantor can sell or transfer property or property rights to another.

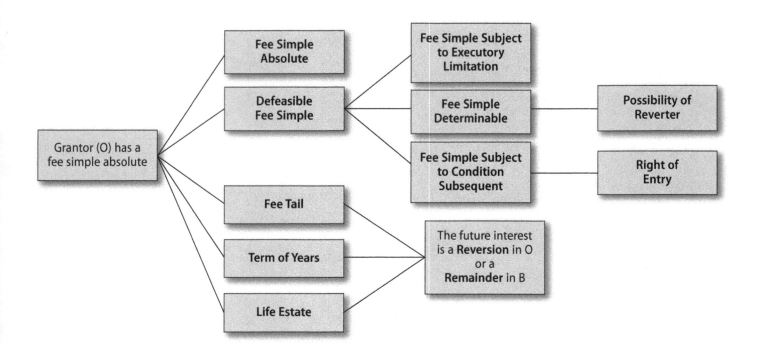

Security Interests in Real Property

A security interest in real property is an interest created by agreement or by operation of law over land to secure the performance of an obligation, usually the payment of a debt.

	Definition	Parties	Arrangement Among Parties	Default
DEED OF TRUST	In exchange for a loan from beneficiary to enable trustor to purchase legal title to land, trustor places legal title to the land in the hands of a trustee who holds title to secure repayment of the loan.	Borrower (trustor). Lender (beneficiary). Neutral third party (trustee).	Trustor has physical possession of the land. Beneficiary has title to the land. Trustee holds title in trust for beneficiary and has the right to foreclose.	If trustor fails to make required payments, trustee is empowered to sell the land and pay beneficiary the monetary proceeds to satisfy the debt. Any surplus is returned to trustor. Trustee's right to sell the land is called foreclosure by **power of sale**, and can be exercised without the need of going to court.
MORTGAGE	In exchange for a loan from mortgagee to enable the purchase of legal title to land, mortgagor places legal title to the land in the name of mortgagee as security for the repayment of the loan.	Borrower (mortgagor). Lender (mortgagee).	Mortgagor has physical possession of the land. Mortgagee has title to the land. Mortgagee has the right to foreclose.	If mortgagor fails to make her required mortgage payments, mortgagee can foreclose on the mortgage by forcing the sale of the land and obtaining the monetary proceeds, or obtaining the land itself at a **judicial foreclosure sale**. A judicial foreclosure sale is ordered by a court and usually conducted by the sheriff.
INSTALLMENT LAND CONTRACT	In exchange for seller financing the purchase of land, seller retains legal title to the land as security for the repayment of the purchase price by buyer. In turn, buyer pays seller in installments until the price is paid, at which point seller transfer title to buyer.	Seller. Buyer.	Buyer has physical possession of the land. Seller has title to the land. Seller has the right to foreclose.	If buyer fails to make payments, seller can usually avoid the foreclosure process by obtaining the land through a process called **forfeiture**. Since buyer does not have title to the land, seller can forfeit the contract, keep all of the money that buyer already paid and take back possession of the land.

Common Interest Developments

Common interest developments ("CIDs") are comprised of separate units in addition to shared facilities and common areas. CIDs are usually created by a developer, and may be modified or amended to meet the community's needs. CIDs are generally governed by an association comprised of individual members, most often through an elected board.

	Home Owners Associations	Condominiums	Cooperatives
UNIT OWNERSHIP	Tenant has a deed and owns her own lot.	Tenant (aka unit owner) has a deed and owns real property.	Tenant (aka shareholder) has a stock certificate and owns shares in a corporation, the business of which is ownership of the cooperative.
COMMON AREA OWNERSHIP	Common areas are owned by the Home Owners Association itself.	Everyone owns the common areas as tenants in common. Each unit owner has an undivided interest in the common elements.	Corporation owns everything.
NAME OF MONTHLY CHARGES	Home Owners Association fees.	Common Charges.	Maintenance.
GOVERNING BODY	Board of Directors.	Board of Managers.	Board of Directors.
CONTROLLING DOCUMENTS	By-Laws. Covenants, Conditions, and Restrictions (CC&Rs). Rules and Regulations (aka House Rules).	Offering Plan. Declaration. By-Laws. Rules and Regulations (aka House Rules).	Offering Plan. Articles of Incorporation. By-Laws. Rules and Regulations (aka House Rules). Proprietary Lease.
REAL ESTATE TAXES	Each lot is on its own tax lot and taxes are paid by individual lot owners directly to the municipality.	Each unit has its own tax lot and taxes are paid by individual unit owners directly to the municipality.	The whole cooperative is on a single tax lot. Shareholders pay the taxes of the building as part of their monthly maintenance fees.
ADMISSIONS PROCESS	Board cannot reject a sale, but it can assert its **Right of First Refusal** and buy for itself a lot being sold by the owner, at the same price and with the same terms as it is being offered.	Board cannot reject a sale, but it can assert its **Right of First Refusal** and buy for itself a unit being sold by the owner, at the same price and with the same terms as it is being offered.	Board can interview applicant and can accept or reject any applicant for any non-discriminatory reason.
UNDERLYING MORTGAGE	No underlying mortgages for Home Owners Associations.	No underlying mortgages for Condominiums.	Underlying mortgage on the whole cooperative is possible.

Torts

Classifications of Torts

A tort is a wrongful act or an infringement of a right to another person's person, property or reputation for which the injured party can seek compensation.

	Definition	Specific Claims	
NEGLIGENCE	A tort resulting from the failure of defendant to exercise reasonable care under the circumstances in fulfilling a duty owed.	Negligence.	
INTENTIONAL TORTS	A civil wrong resulting from actions intentionally committed by defendant. Note that in tort law, the term "intentional" focuses on the voluntariness of the action, rather than a defendant's mens rea as under criminal law.	Assault. Battery. Intentional infliction of emotional distress.	False imprisonment. Trespass to land. Trespass to chattel. Conversion.
STRICT LIABILITY	Liability that is imposed upon an actor regardless of culpability.	Abnormally dangerous activities. Workers' compensation.	Wild or vicious animals. Products liability.
DEFAMATION	Defendant makes a statement of or concerning plaintiff, which is harmful to plaintiff's reputation and which is communicated to a third party.	Libel.	Slander.
PRIVACY TORTS	The law protects against arbitrary interferences with a person's privacy, family, home or correspondence, and attacks upon honor or reputation.	Misappropriation. Intrusion.	False Light. Public Disclosure.
NUISANCE	An interference with use and enjoyment of property. Nuisances are most commonly in the form of disturbing noises, objectionable odors, smoke or other kinds of pollution.	Public nuisance.	Private nuisance.
MISREPRESENTATION	Action for damages that arises when a person justifiably relies on another's statement, made with recklessness as to its truth, or with knowledge that it is false or misleading, intending for the recipient to have relied on the statement.	Negligent misrepresentation.	Intentional misrepresentation.
INTENTIONAL INTERFERENCE WITH BUSINESS RELATIONS	Action for damages as a result of defendant's knowing and intentional interference with plaintiff's contractual or other business relationships or activities.	Injurious falsehood. Interference with existing contracts.	Interference with business expectancy.
WRONGFUL INSTITUTION OF LEGAL PROCEEDINGS	Action for damages that can be brought by someone who was a victim of misuse of the court system.	Malicious prosecution. Wrongful institution of civil proceedings.	Abuse of process.

Elements of the Tort of Negligence

Plaintiff must prove that: (1) defendant was under a legal duty to act in a particular fashion, (2) defendant breached this duty by failing to conform her behavior accordingly, (3) plaintiff suffered injury or loss, (4) as a consequence of defendant's breach of duty.

Element	Definition	Test
DUTY	The obligation to all foreseeable persons to exercise reasonable care under the circumstances.	Determination of one's duty is made through usage of an objective test, which considers how a hypothetical **reasonably prudent person** in defendant's position would have acted under the same circumstances, considering the reasonably foreseeable risk and probability of harm to others.
BREACH	There is a breach of duty when an individual fails to meet its obligation to act reasonably.	A demonstration that the defendant did not conform her conduct to that of a reasonably prudent person under the circumstances.
CAUSATION	Close causal connection between the breach of duty complained of and the injury suffered.	Defendant's failure to act with reasonable care must be shown to be: (1) the **actual cause in fact** ("but-for" cause) of the injury to the plaintiff, AND (2) defendant's act of negligence was the **proximate cause** of the harm suffered.
DAMAGES	Resulting loss.	It must be shown that **actual damages** (*i.e., physical injury or financial loss*) were suffered. Nominal damages and punitive damages are generally unavailable.

The Reasonable Person Test to Determine Negligence

To determine whether a duty of care has been violated, what that level of care is needs to be established. Generally, the reasonable person standard applies. It compares the inferred behavior of a hypothetical person of ordinary prudence in the same position and situation as the defendant, to determine whether the defendant acted negligently.

Factors	Rule	Exception?	Standard Used	Examples
PHYSICAL CHARACTER-ISTICS	The reasonable person is considered to have the same physical attributes as defendant.	✔	What a reasonably prudent person with the same physique (height, weight, sex) would do.	*A 5' tall woman weighing 95 lbs. failed to remove a loose board, which later injured someone, because she lacked the physical strength to do so. The standard of negligence will be what a reasonably prudent 5' tall, 95 lb. woman would do.*
PHYSICAL DISABILITIES	If the defendant has a physical disability, the standard for negligence is what a reasonably prudent person with that physical disability would do.	✔	What a reasonably prudent person with the same physical disability would do.	*A blind or deaf person will be judged by a standard that considers what a reasonably prudent blind or deaf person sharing the same disability would have done, seen or been aware of under the same or similar circumstances.*
INDIVIDUAL TEMPERAMENT	The reasonably prudent person is NOT necessarily considered to be subject to the same temperament.	✘	Reasonable person standard applies.	*Kip was quick-tempered, and became angry when a machine malfunctioned. He ignored the sparks flying from that machine, and stormed out of the factory. The machine caught fire and killed a factory worker. Being quick-tempered or of poorer judgment than the ordinary person will not absolve Kip of negligence.*
MENTAL ILLNESS	The reasonably prudent person does not recognize mental illness.	✘	Reasonable person standard applies.	*A schizophrenic will be subject to the same liability for a car accident that results from his having removed a stop sign in an intersection because voices in his head directed him to do so, as would a person not suffering from schizophrenia.*
INFANCY	The reasonably prudent person is considered to be a child if defendant is a child.	✔	What a reasonably prudent child of the same age, intelligence and experience would do.	*A 6-year-old boy who pushes a victim into the shallow end of a pool thereby causing injury is subject to the standard of a reasonably prudent 6-year-old, rather than a reasonably prudent person.*
INTOXICATION	Voluntary intoxication does not excuse negligent acts performed while intoxicated. Involuntary intoxication may cause conduct that would otherwise be considered negligent.	✘	Reasonable person standard applies.	*A drunk skier lost control of himself and crashed into a bystander. Being drunk will not excuse the skier; instead the skier's conduct will be judged by that of a reasonably prudent sober person.*
SPECIAL TRAINING OR KNOWLEDGE	If defendant has special knowledge or training, defendant is held to a higher standard of care.	✔	What a reasonably prudent person with the same specialized knowledge or training would do.	*An electrician whose work causes a fire will be judged by what a reasonably prudent electrician should have done, rather than the standard of a reasonably prudent person.*

The Reasonable Person Test to Determine Negligence, *continued*

Factors	Rule	Exception?	Standard Used	Examples
CUSTOMS	Evidence of a specific activity that is routinely carried out in a community or industry can be used to show the presence or absence of reasonable care by defendant, although such evidence is not dispositive. The fact that a whole community acts negligently may not necessarily excuse conduct, but rather may indicate the whole community behaves in a negligent manner.	✔	A court may consider what a reasonably prudent member of defendant's community or industry would do.	*A man is running on the treadmill at the gym and suffers a heart attack and dies. A defibrillator would have saved the runners life, but as is customary with the gyms in the area, and in compliance with local regulations, the gym did not have such an instrument. The fact that most gyms do not have defibrillators will not necessarily excuse the gym for failure to have a defibrillator, but it will be considered evidence supporting that this gym's failure to maintain such an instrument on the premises was not negligent.*
EMERGENCIES	The reasonably prudent person in an emergency will not be required to exercise the same judgment and care as a person who has ample time to reflect and react, provided that the person did not cause the emergency.	✔	What a reasonably prudent person in an emergency situation would do.	*A man is speeding to get his wife, who has been shot in the chest, to the hospital. The man hits a pedestrian. The man's conduct will be judged in accordance with that of an individual responding to an emergency, rather than that of the reasonably prudent person.*

The Duty Element of Negligence

Generally, a duty of reasonable care is owed to all foreseeable plaintiffs to protect against harm to their physical safety or damage to their property. Negligence occurs when there is a breach of a duty that occurs with actual and proximate cause, and results in damages.

	Definition	Rule	Result	Example
NONFEASANCE	Passive inaction or a failure to act to protect another from harm.	An individual will generally not be held liable in tort solely for failure to act unless they are under a legal duty to perform.	A failure to benefit the plaintiff.	*If Alan sees Mike drowning in the pool, he does not have a duty to rescue him unless he is legally obligated to protect Mike's safety.*
MISFEASANCE	Affirmative conduct injuring another.	Liability for misfeasance arises when the duty to act reasonably towards another is violated by affirmative acts that endanger the victim or their property.	A risk of harm to the plaintiff is created.	*Amy hit a pedestrian while driving under the influence of alcohol and amphetamines. Amy will be found negligent for any injuries suffered by the pedestrian from having been hit by the car Amy was driving.*

When Is There a Duty to Act?

An individual will generally not be held liable in tort solely for failure to act, except in the following circumstances.

	Rule	Examples
SPECIAL RELATIONSHIP	When there is a special relationship between the parties.	*A common carrier with its passengers. An employer with its employees.* *An innkeeper with its guests. A landlord with its tenants.* *A school with its students. A parent to its minor child.*
CONTRACTUAL OBLIGATION	If a person has a duty to perform under a contract and fails to perform the contractual obligation with due care.	*An amusement park hired an engineer to do monthly inspections of its roller coaster. In June, the engineer inspected the roller coaster carelessly resulting in a rider's injury. The engineer is liable to the rider.*
ASSUMPTION OF DUTY	Even where there is no legal obligation to act, once a person begins to render assistance to another, a duty is created and the person rendering assistance must proceed with reasonable care.	*If Kara sees Scott drowning in the pool, she does not have a duty to rescue him. However, if Kara throws a life preserver into the pool, she will now be subject to a duty to continue to use reasonable care in trying to rescue him.*
DUTY TO CONTROL OTHERS' ACTIONS	If a person has a duty to control third parties, that person can be liable in negligence for failing to exercise that control over a third party who causes harm as a result of the lack of oversight.	*Parent was advised that her daughter was bullying another girl at school. Despite several notices and conferences between Parent and school staff, Parent dismissed the concerns as being an overreaction, and did little to attempt to change daughter's behavior. Parent will be liable for any harm done to girl by her daughter.*
CREATION OF PERIL	When an individual negligently places a person in danger, that individual has an affirmative duty to take reasonable action to prevent further harm by rendering care or aid.	*While simultaneously texting and driving, Driver hit a pedestrian who was crossing the street. Pedestrian was caused to fall into the middle of the street. Driver has an affirmative obligation to stop and assist or make reasonable efforts to obtain assistance for pedestrian.*
CO-VENTURES	When a person is engaged with another who becomes injured during a common pursuit, the person is under a duty to exercise reasonable care to prevent further harm by rendering care or aid.	*Melanie and David are mountain climbing when David's cord snaps and he falls 100 ft. Melanie has a duty to make reasonable efforts to aid David or seek assistance for him because they are engaged in a co-venture.*

Duty of Landowners to Those on the Premises
Whether a landowner owes a duty to a person who enters onto her land depends on the legal status of the entrant.

Status of Entrant		Definition	Rule	Duties Owed		
				Artificial Conditions	Natural Conditions	Active Operations
TRESPASSERS	UNDISCOVERED TRESPASSERS	One who enters land without permission and whose presence is unknown to the landowner.	Landowner owes no duty to an undiscovered trespasser.	✘	✘	✘
	ANTICIPATED TRESPASSERS	One who is known to enter upon a limited portion of landowner's property.	Once landowner has knowledge that a particular person is trespassing, landowner is then under a duty to exercise reasonable care to warn the trespasser of, or to make safe, artificial conditions known to the landowner that involve a risk of serious injury or death and that the trespasser is unlikely to discover.	Duty to warn of, or make safe, known conditions if not obvious and highly dangerous.	✘	Duty of Reasonable Care.
	CHILDREN	A child who enters a landowner's property without permission.	Landowner owes a child trespasser the duty to exercise ordinary care when landowner knows that children are likely to trespass and that a condition exists on the land that the child does not realize is dangerous. Under the **attractive nuisance doctrine**, a landowner with an artificial condition known to be appealing to children, which poses a risk of death or serious injury, the danger of which children are unlikely to appreciate due to their youth, has a duty to exercise reasonable care to protect the children from harm provided the burden of eliminating or protecting against the danger is slight compared to the risk.	Duty to warn of, or make safe, if foreseeable risk to child outweighs the expense of eliminating danger.	✘	Duty of Reasonable Care.
LICENSEES		A person who is on the owner's land with permission, but is not there for the landowners benefit. (*i.e., social guest*)	Landowner has a duty to warn the licensee of or make safe any known natural or artificial conditions that could harm the licensee. Landowner does not have an affirmative duty to inspect the premises for dangerous conditions.	Duty to warn of, or make safe, known conditions if not obvious and dangerous.	Duty to warn of, or make safe, known conditions if not obvious and dangerous.	Duty of Reasonable Care.
INVITEES		Any member of the public who is on the premises with permission from the landowner for a purpose connected with the use of the premises. (*i.e., business patron*)	Landowner has a duty to warn the invitee of or make safe all known natural or artificial conditions that could harm the invitee and to inspect the premises for dangerous conditions.	Duty to make reasonable inspections to discover non-obvious dangerous conditions and warn of or make them safe.	Duty to make reasonable inspections to discover non-obvious dangerous conditions and warn of or make them safe.	Duty of Reasonable Care.

The Breach of Duty Element of Negligence

To prove breach, plaintiff must establish defendant failed to conform her behavior in accordance with her obligations.

Methods of Proof	Definition	Examples
CUSTOM OR USAGE	Evidence of a custom or generally accepted routine carried out in a community or industry can be used to demonstrate the presence or absence of reasonable care by the defendant. Evidence of custom or usage is a consideration but not definitive proof of the presence or absence of a breach of duty.	*Adam runs a recreational center with a rock climbing wall. It is customary in the industry to permit climbers to adjust their own harness before beginning a rock climb. Adam's customer, a first time climber, failed to properly secure her harness and fell to the ground. Customer sued Adam's recreational center for negligence in not properly causing her to be secured into the harness. Adam offered into evidence the industry custom of having customers secure themselves. Although the custom in the industry is not dispositive, the court may consider the evidence in determining whether a duty was breached.*
RES IPSA LOQUITUR	"The thing speaks for itself." A rebuttable presumption of negligence under circumstances in which: defendant was in sole control of the instrumentality of the harm AND the complained of injury would not ordinarily occur in the absence of negligence.	*A load of bricks on the roof of a vacant building being constructed by Construction Co. falls and injures Andy, a pedestrian walking on the sidewalk adjacent to the building. Construction Co. is liable in negligence under a theory of res ipsa loquitur because it was in sole control of the building, and bricks don't fall off of buildings without the presence of negligence.* *CONTRAST* *A load of bricks on the roof of an occupied building being renovated by Construction Co. falls and injures Andy, a pedestrian walking on the sidewalk adjacent to the building. Construction Co. is NOT automatically liable in negligence under a theory of res ipsa loquitur because it was NOT in sole control of the building, and thus, plaintiff will have to demonstrate Construction Co.'s responsibility for placing the bricks on the roof and their negligence in causing said bricks to fall in order to make out a prima facie case for negligence.*
NEGLIGENCE PER SE	Presumption that a duty has been breached under circumstances in which a defendant violated a statute intended to protect the plaintiff. Not a per se case of negligence, which still requires the proof of causation and damages.	*Driving faster than the speed limit establishes prima facie evidence that a duty was breached in a case where an automobile accident is the result.* *The law prohibiting driving in excess of a certain speed can be used as prima evidence that defendant breached a duty, leaving only the elements of causation and damages to be proven.*

The Causation Element of Negligence

Actual and proximate causation must be demonstrated to support a claim for negligence.

	Types of Cases	Rule	Test	Examples	
ACTUAL ("BUT FOR") CAUSATION	Determinable Cause of Injury and Defendant	An act or omission is the cause in fact of an injury if the injury would not have occurred **but for** the defendant's negligence.	"But For" Test	*A captain did not bring life vests aboard his boat before he took his passengers to sea. One passenger who was unable to swim, fell overboard and drowned. The passenger would not have drowned but for the captain's failure to bring the life vests.*	To support a claim of negligence, the plaintiff must first show a causal link between defendant's action and plaintiff's injury.
	Concurrent Causes of Injury	If there is more than one cause of injury to the plaintiff, where defendant is a **substantial factor** in bringing about the injury, actual causation is present.	Substantial Factor Test	*Two oil companies are drilling near a lake. Leakage from rigs owned by each company pollutes the lake. The property owner sues Oil Co. A. Because the damage caused by each company was sufficient to pollute the property, Oil Co. A will be liable because it is a substantial factor causing the property damage.*	
	Multiple Defendants at Fault	If there are two (or more) defendants determined to have been possible causes of the injury, but plaintiff is unable to make that determination with certainty, the burden of proof shifts to the defendants to demonstrate they were not the actual causes of the injury. Absent such proof, each defendant can be held liable.	Alternative Liability Test	*Two hunters negligently fire shots into a forest, one of which hits victim. The burden shifts to each of the defendants to demonstrate it was not their bullet that hit the victim. If neither can demonstrate lack of fault, both will be liable for the injuries.*	
PROXIMATE CAUSATION	Direct Cause	If there is a determinable, uninterrupted chain of events between defendant's negligent conduct and plaintiff's injury, and plaintiff's injury is a **foreseeable consequence** of defendant's conduct, proximate cause exists.	Foreseeability Test	*A captain was speeding in his motorboat and hit a huge rock jutting out of the water. As a result, one of the passengers fell out of the boat and drowned. Hitting the rock and the drowning were a foreseeable result of speeding.*	Once actual causation has been established, plaintiff must show her injuries were a foreseeable consequence of defendant's actions.
	Indirect Cause	When an external event occurs after defendant's negligent act and helps cause injury to plaintiff, proximate cause will be established so long as the **intervening external event** would have been foreseeable to a reasonable person. Otherwise, it may be found that the intervening external event supersedes defendant's action and defendant will not be liable.	Intervening Cause Test	*If a landlord fails to get the lock on the front door of a house fixed and then the house gets burglarized, the landlord will be liable to its tenant because a burglary was foreseeable.* *If an arsonist burns down the house and kills all of the tenants, the landlord will not be liable even though she was negligent for not fixing the door, because it was unforeseeable that an arsonist would burn down the house.*	

Professional Standards Used in Medical Malpractice Cases

Defendants with special knowledge or training are held to a higher standard of care from that of the average reasonably prudent person. The following standards are used by courts to determine whether a defendant medical professional acted negligently.

Standard	Rule	Purpose	Issues	Usage
STRICT LOCALITY STANDARD	A professional is held to the standards of practice in the community in which she practices.	The purpose is to hold professionals to a standard of care similar to other professionals in the area. In the past, professional standards varied significantly between communities.	In small or remote communities, a defendant might be the only practitioner to judge the conduct against.	No longer used.
SIMILAR LOCALITY STANDARD	A professional is held to the standards of others practicing in similar communities with similar facilities available. The professional's conduct is measured against others with similar training, similar backgrounds, and from a similar locality.	The purpose was to broaden the pool of applicable professionals to increase the willingness of professionals to testify against one another while still making allowances for differences between areas.	Professionals are often reluctant to testify against each other.	Used by a minority of modern courts.
NATIONAL STANDARD	The professional is held to a national standard regardless of the area in which they practice.	The purpose is to maximize the likelihood that plaintiff will fulfill her burden of producing expert testimony by calling on experts from all of the country.	Very few issues since professional education has become more uniform nationally.	Used by most modern courts.

The Damages Element of Negligence

To prove negligence, defendant's conduct must have caused injury to plaintiff, her property, or her rights.

Types of Damages		Definition	When Awarded	Examples
COMPENSATORY DAMAGES	**PHYSICAL DISTRESS**	Monetary compensation for past, present and future physical loss or harm suffered by plaintiff as a result of plaintiff's physical injury.	Personal injury claims. Negligent infliction of emotional distress claims.	*Lost earnings.* *Medical expenses.*
	EMOTIONAL DISTRESS	Monetary compensation for past, present and future emotional loss or harm suffered by plaintiff as a result of plaintiff's physical injury.	Personal injury claims. Negligent infliction of emotional distress claims.	*Pain and suffering.* *Loss of consortium.*
	PROPERTY DAMAGE	Monetary compensation for past, present and future loss or harm suffered by plaintiff as a result of damage to plaintiff's property.	Property damage claims.	*Fair market value of an item at the time of the accident OR the reasonable cost of repair.*
PUNITIVE DAMAGES		Monetary compensation awarded to an injured party that goes beyond that which is necessary to compensate the individual for injury or loss and is intended to punish defendant's wrongful conduct and to deter defendant and others from similar conduct in the future.	Negligence claims where the defendant's conduct was willful and wanton, reckless or malicious. Products liability claims.	*Punitive damages may be awarded to a victim injured in a car accident after her gas tank explodes, if it is demonstrated the car manufacturer was on notice of the likelihood the gas tank could explode upon impact.*

Affirmative Defenses in Negligence Actions

The following are potential affirmative defenses that can be raised by defendant to shield herself from liability.

		Definition	Examples
CONTRIBUTORY NEGLIGENCE		Conduct on the part of plaintiff that contributes proximately to her injuries. It is a complete bar to recovery in a Contributory Negligence jurisdiction unless defendant had the "Last Clear Chance" to avoid the accident, in which case the liability for the injury shifts back to defendant.	Plaintiff was crossing the street against the light and was hit and killed by a speeding car. Regardless of the degree of the driver's culpability for the accident, so long as the plaintiff was partially responsible, she will be barred from recovery in a Contributory Negligence jurisdiction. **Exception:** If plaintiff can successfully demonstrate defendant was the party in the position of having the last clear chance to avoid the accident, in which case the responsibility and liability for the accident shifts back to defendant.
COMPARATIVE NEGLIGENCE	**Pure Comparative Negligence**	A negligent plaintiff is able to recover even if her negligence exceeds that of defendant in a Pure Comparative Negligence jurisdiction; plaintiff's damages in accordance with her proportionate share of liability.	Plaintiff suffers $100,000 worth of damage. A jury finds that plaintiff was 60% at fault and defendant was 40% at fault. Plaintiff will recover $40,000 ($100,000 minus 60% of $100,000).
	Partial Comparative Negligence	In a Partial Comparative Negligence jurisdiction, plaintiff's negligence is a complete bar to recovery in instances in which plaintiff is more than 50% liable. Where plaintiff is 50% or less liable, her negligence proportionately reduces plaintiff's recovery.	Plaintiff suffers $100,000 worth of damage. A jury finds that plaintiff was 60% at fault and defendant was 40% at fault. Plaintiff will recover nothing since her fault was greater than the defendants. However, if defendant were 60% at fault and plaintiff 40% at fault, plaintiff would recover for 60% of her injuries.
STATUTE OF LIMITATIONS		A time limitation on bringing a claim against a defendant for harm or loss suffered.	A victim's wife was barred from suing the man who hit and killed her husband with his car because she waited five years before instituting a lawsuit in a jurisdiction in which the statute of limitations for a wrongful death claim was two years. The action is time barred, and will be dismissed.
IMMUNITIES		Due to public policy considerations, a group of people or entities are thought to require special protections under certain circumstances even at the expense of those injured by its tortious acts.	Family immunity. (Note that most states have eliminated the bar on family members suing one another for negligence). Charitable immunity. (Note that most states have eliminated the bar on individuals suing charities for negligence). Sovereign immunity.
ASSUMPTION OF RISK	**Express Assumption of Risk**	Knowing, voluntary and expressed understanding by plaintiff that a risk is being assumed. Often arises in a contractual limitation on liability.	Before going skydiving, James signs a waiver in which he agrees not to sue the skydiving company if he is injured. James has expressly assumed the risk.
	Implied Assumption of Risk	Plaintiff is barred from recovery if plaintiff's conduct demonstrates an awareness and understanding of the risk engaged in.	A firefighter who was injured in a house fire will be barred from recovering for her burns since she was injured while carrying out normal rescue duties.

Defendant's State of Mind During the Commission of a Tort

An intentional tort is a wrongful act or an infringement of a right leading to a legal liability
that was brought about by defendant's intentional conduct.

State of Mind	Definition	Intent	Rule	Example
INTENT TO COMMIT A TORT	A person desires to cause a particular act upon another person or another's property.	Intentional.	The intent must be to cause some act on another or another's property regardless of whether the actor intended to cause harm.	*Bill intentionally punches Jon in the face.*
INTENT TO COMMIT A DIFFERENT TORT	A person desires to commit one act, but actually commits another.	Intentional.	A person who intends to commit one tort but actually commits another is liable for the tort committed.	*Erin pretends to slap Matt intending to scare him, but actually hits and injures him. Erin is liable for battery, despite intending to cause an assault.*
SUBSTANTIAL CERTAINTY THAT A TORT WILL OCCUR	A person does not know that a tort will definitely result from her actions, but is almost certain that it will.	Intentional.	A person's actions are considered intentional even if the actor did not desire the specific result, but knew with substantial certainty that it would occur as a result of her actions.	*Kim put oil on the tiles of the bathroom floor. She was not positive that this would make Hollie slip, but she was almost certain it would.*
POSSIBLE THAT A TORT WILL OCCUR	A person does not know with substantial certainty that a tort will result from her actions, but such a result has a chance of occurring.	Unintentional.	An intentional tort is not committed if a person's act might cause injury to another person when committed, but it could give rise to a negligence claim if the actor failed to meet a reasonable standard of care for someone of the same age.	*Nicki loosened one of the legs on Brandon's chair. She was not sure whether the chair would break when Brandon sat down, but she knew that there was an increased chance it would.*
TRANSFERRED INTENT	A person intends to commit a tort against one person, but actually injures another person. Transferred intent only applies to assault, battery, false imprisonment, and trespass.	Intentional.	If a person has the necessary intent to commit an intentional tort against one person, she will be held to have committed an intentional tort against anyone who was injured by her actions.	*Randi intends to shoot Laurie, but misses and the bullet hits Adam.*
NO INTENT TO HARM	A person intends to commit an action but does not intend to cause injury.	Intentional.	A person will have the intent necessary for an intentional tort if she intentionally performs a tortious act without the desire to injure another.	*Blake playfully punched Gregg when she saw a Volkswagen Beetle drive by. Although she intended to punch Gregg, she did not desire to hurt him.*

Intentional Torts

An intentional tort is a wrongful act or an infringement of a right leading to a legal liability.
Requires proof of act, intent, and causation.

	Definition	Available Defenses		Transferred Intent
ASSAULT	Intentional act causing another to reasonably fear immediate harm or offensive contact.	Consent. Self-defense.	Defense of others. Defense of property.	✔
BATTERY	Intentional act causing harmful or offensive contact with another.	Consent. Self-defense.	Defense of others. Defense of property.	✔
FALSE IMPRISONMENT	Intentional restraint of another in a bounded area.	Consent. Self-defense. Defense of others.	Defense of property. Shopkeeper's privilege.	✔
INTENTIONAL INFLICTION OF EMOTIONAL DISTRESS	Extreme or reckless conduct that intentionally or recklessly causes severe emotion distress in another.	Consent. Self-defense.	Defense of others. Defense of property.	✘
TRESPASS TO LAND	Intentional, physical invasion onto another's land.	Consent. Self-defense. Defense of others.	Defense of property. Public necessity. Private necessity.	✔
TRESPASS TO CHATTEL	Intentional interference with another's right of possession to personal property by taking away or damaging the property.	Consent. Self-defense. Defense of others.	Defense of property. Public necessity. Private necessity.	✔
CONVERSION	Intentional interference with another's right of possession to personal property by taking away or damaging the property in a way that is serious enough to warrant payment of full market value of the property.	Consent. Self-defense. Defense of others.	Defense of property. Public necessity. Private necessity.	✘

Assault and Battery

An intentional tort is a wrongful act or an infringement of a right leading to a legal liability that was brought about by defendant's intentional conduct. Assault and battery are examples of intentional torts.

	Definition	Intent	Effect	Damages	Example
ASSAULT	The creation of apprehension of imminent bodily injury in the victim OR attempted battery.	A person must intend to cause apprehension of contact in another person or intend to make actual contact with another.	Assault requires at a minimum that an imminent apprehension of harm has occurred, or an incomplete battery.	**Nominal damages** may be available for a victim who can establish that another person had intentional harmful or offensive contact with them, even if the victim was not physically injured or did not incur financial loss. **Compensatory damages** may be available for the victim's mental suffering and or any physical injury resulting from the assault. **Punitive damages** may be available to the victim if the actor's conduct was outrageous or malicious.	*If Adam swings a bat and hits Kevin, he has committed the tort of assault, as well as battery.* *If Felice swings a bat at Kevin and misses because Kevin jumps out of the way, Felice will have committed the tort of assault, but not battery.*
BATTERY	The intentional infliction of a harmful OR offensive bodily contact.	A person must intend to assault or put fear of imminent, harmful or offensive conduct in another.	Battery requires at a minimum that a harmful or offensive touching has taken place.	**Nominal damages** may be available for a victim who can establish intentional harmful or offensive contact, even if the victim was not actually physically injured or did not incur financial loss. **Compensatory damages** may be available for pain, suffering, embarrassment or a mental effect, even if the victim was not physically injured. **Punitive damages** may be available to the victim if the actor's conduct was outrageous or malicious.	*Claire intentionally shoots Adam in the foot.* *Claire intends to shoot Adam in the foot, but misses. Claire has not committed a battery since there was no harmful or offensive contact with Adam's body.*

Trespass

An intentional tort is a wrongful act or an infringement of a right leading to a legal liability that was brought about by defendant's intentional conduct. Trespass is an intentional tort. Trespass is the intentional interference with the property of another.

Type	Definition	Intent	Damages	Examples
TRESPASS TO LAND	Intentionally entering onto or remaining on another's land without permission; or intentionally causing another person or object to enter onto another's land without permission.	A person is liable for trespass if she purposefully enters onto or remains on the land of another, or purposefully causes another person or object to enter the land without permission. Mistake is not a defense.	No proof of actual damages required. Nominal, Punitive and Actual/Compensatory damages are available. The measure of actual damages may include consideration of the diminution of market value, cost of restoration, loss of use, physical injury, emotional distress, and the resulting discomfort or annoyance.	*While Jessica and Paul are walking, Jessica pushes Paul onto another person's property.* *Paul has NOT committed a trespass because he neither intended to enter the land, nor did he intend to cause a physical invasion. His action was involuntary and thus not intentional.* *Jessica is a trespasser because Jessica caused Paul to enter the property. Her intent to cause Paul to physically invade the land qualifies her actions as trespass.*
TRESPASS TO CHATTEL	An intentional interference with the use or possession of another's personal property.	A person is liable for trespass to chattel if she intentionally interferes with another's possession of property, there need not be an intent to cause damages.	Damages required. The measure can be the amount of damage to the chattel; or loss of use.	*Jill dents the door of Jack's car. Jill is liable for trespass to chattel and Jack can recover damages for the cost of repairing the door.*
CONVERSION	An intentional interference with the use or possession of another's personal property that is so severe that it cannot be returned or repaired to its original state. Requires the converter to pay full value of the item. The distinction between conversion and trespass to chattel is based on the severity of the damage.	A person is liable for conversion if she intentionally interferes with another's possession of property, there need not be an intent to cause damages.	Damages required. The measure of damages is the full value of the property prior to its conversion.	*Danielle set fire to Jeff's boat. Danielle is liable for conversion and Jeff can recover the full market value of the boat.*

Conversion

The intentional interference with the use or possession of another's property. The level of damages distinguishes conversion from trespass to chattel. An act will be conversion if it was so severe that it requires the converter to pay the full replacement value of the item.

	Examples	Conversion	Trespass to Chattel
PURCHASE OF A STOLEN ITEM	Allyson buys stolen baseball cards from Ben.	✔	✘
FRAUDULENTLY OBTAINING AN ITEM	Jon persuades Becky to give him her television by misleading her into believing she cannot keep her television in her new dormitory.	✔	✘
BAILMENT OF A LOST OR STOLEN ITEM	A coat check room attendant stores a stolen fur coat given to her by a patron.	✘	✘
TRANSPORTATION OF AN ITEM	Todd moves Laura's teddy bear from her room to his room next door.	✘	✔
TRANSPORTATION OF AN ITEM INTO A RESTRICTED LOCATION	Sophie moves Sam's guitar from his room into a locked storage facility.	✔	✘
WITHHOLDING OF AN ITEM	Dave borrows Bryan's shovel and refuses to return it until after the winter.	✔	✘
FUNDAMENTAL MODIFICATION OF AN ITEM	Jamie alters Annie's long-sleeve dress to make it sleeveless.	✔	✘
MINOR ALTERATION OF AN ITEM	Jessie sews a tiny hole in Blair's shirt.	✘	✘
SHORT TERM BORROWING OF AN ITEM	Hallie borrows her mom's shirt to go to a party.	✘	✔
DESTRUCTION OF AN ITEM	Spencer cuts the strings of Marley's tennis racquet.	✔	✘
EXTREME USE OF OR DAMAGE TO AN ITEM	Nicki wears out the tires on Randi's car.	✔	✘
ASSERTION OF OWNERSHIP OVER AN ITEM	Martin is tells everyone that Josie's computer is really his computer.	✘	✘

Infliction of Emotional Distress

Infliction of emotional distress is a tort claim for conduct that results in severe emotional distress. The conduct can be either intentional or as a result of negligence.

	Conduct	Elements	Fault	Causation & Damages	Notes
INTENTIONAL INFLICTION OF EMOTIONAL DISTRESSS	Defendant's behavior must be extreme or and outrageous.	(1) Defendant acts intentionally, (2) Defendant's conduct is extreme or outrageous, (3) Plaintiff suffers severe emotional distress.	Defendant must intentionally act to cause severe emotional distress; OR Defendant must recklessly disregard the high likelihood that emotional distress will occur.	Defendant's act must cause severe emotional distress.	No physical symptoms are required. Demonstration of severe emotional distress is sufficient.
NEGLIGENT INFLICTION OF EMOTIONAL DISTRESSS (NIED)	Defendant must subject plaintiff to severe emotional distress likely to cause physical symptoms, OR subject plaintiff to the threat of physical injury. Also includes tampering with a corpse and misinforming an individual that a close family member has died.	(1) Defendant engaged in negligent conduct, (2) Plaintiff is present in the "zone of danger" when the injury occurs, (3) Plaintiff suffers emotional distress that is accompanied by physical manifestation of harm. *Note:* Some states require Plaintiff in an NIED claim to be the victim of the negligence or an immediate family member only. *Note:* Claims involving tampering with a corpse or misinforming that a family member has died do not require proof of "zone of danger" or physical manifestation of emotional distress.	Defendant's conduct must be negligent.	Defendant's acts must cause emotional distress that manifests itself physically. *Exception:* where plaintiff also suffered physical injury as a result of defendant's negligence, or the negligent act involves tampering with a corpse or misinforming a plaintiff about a family member's death.	NIED can be a second tort claim for plaintiff seeking recovery for physical injuries resulting from negligence, in which case, there is no requirement that zone of danger and physical manifestations of the emotional distress be proven. Plaintiff's physical injury resulting from the tort is enough to support an NIED claim for the accompanying emotional distress.

Negligent Infliction of Emotional Distress

Negligent infliction of emotional distress is a tort claim for conduct that has caused plaintiff emotional distress that often requires physical manifestation of the emotional harm.

	Test	Rule	Requirements	Example
ZONE OF DANGER	**ZONE OF DANGER**	A plaintiff who has suffered emotional injury because she sustained a physical injury as a result of defendant's negligent act; OR was placed in close proximity to the harm caused to another such that she feared physical injury as a result of defendant's negligent conduct.	The threat must be directed at the plaintiff or someone in her immediate presence. *Note:* Some jurisdictions allow recovery outside the immediate zone of danger if: - they are an immediate family member; - witnessed the injury	*A mother looking out her apartment window sees her child get hit by a negligently driven car.* ***Common Law:*** *she cannot recover for the emotional distress caused by having witnessed the accident because she was not within the target zone.* ***Modern Courts:*** *under state law that has expanded the zone of danger from which recovery is permitted, mother can recover for the emotional distress caused by having witnessed the accident, even though she was not within the immediate zone of danger.*
	BYSTANDER	A plaintiff who suffers emotional injury as a result of witnessing an accident from close proximity to the accident.	(1) Plaintiff must have been present at the scene of the injury, AND (2) Observed the event; AND (3) Suffered emotional distress that manifests itself physically. *Note:* Some jurisdictions require a plaintiff bystander to be an immediate family member.	*Jane and Sid were walking when a negligent driver hit Sid, and almost hit Jane before she was able to jump out of the way. Although Jane herself was not physically injured, she may be able to recover for emotional damages resulting from having been in immediate proximity of the harm.*
	PHYSICAL MANIFESTATION	A plaintiff seeking damages for emotional injury stemming from a negligent act must have suffered a physical manifestation of that emotional injury. *Note:* No such physical manifestation of emotional harm is required where the plaintiff also suffered physical injury as a result of defendant's negligence; or the harm involves tampering with a corpse; or misinforming plaintiff about the death of an immediate family member.	Demonstration of a physical manifestation as a result of the emotional injury.	*A negligent driver causes a violent car accident that is witnessed by the victim's sister, who suffers a heart attack as a result of the shock. The negligent driver may be held responsible for the emotional distress that caused the heart attack.*

Tests to Determine Negligent Infliction of Emotional Distress

Negligent infliction of emotional distress is a tort claim for conduct that has caused plaintiff emotional distress that often requires physical manifestation of the emotional harm. Below are tests to determine whether plaintiff can recover for emotional distress resulting from defendant's negligent acts.

Test	Rule	Requirements	Rationale	Examples	Current Use
PHYSICAL IMPACT TEST	Plaintiff seeking damages for emotional injury stemming from a negligent act must have contemporaneously suffered some physical contact or injury due to defendant's conduct.	Demonstrated physical injury or impact must be shown.	States that employ or employed the physical impact test justified the test as a means of assuring the legitimacy of the negligent infliction of emotional distress claim.	*If Ally is handicapped after being hit by a negligently driven car, she will be able to recover for resulting depression.* *However, the pedestrian bystander who witnessed the injury will be unable to recover for resulting panic attacks.*	Minority of states recognize the physical impact test, and most of those states have numerous exceptions to that rule; only Kentucky uses a pure physical impact test requiring some physical contact or injury as a prerequisite to a negligent infliction of emotional distress claim.
ZONE OF DANGER TEST	Plaintiff can recover for emotional injuries sustained as a result of defendant's negligence provided plaintiff suffered a physical injury as a result of defendant's negligence; OR plaintiff was in close proximity to the physical impact, and suffered emotional distress as a result.	The threat must be directed at plaintiff or someone in her immediate presence.	The degree of emotional injury suffered by a bystander is greater when the claimant is in close proximity to the injured.	*If a negligent driver almost crashes into Jane, but she is able to jump out of the way, Jane may still be able to recover for the emotional damages that resulted from the fear of almost being struck.*	Used by courts, but the modern trend is towards expanding the availability of recovery for emotional distress to those nearby, but not necessarily within the traditional zone of danger.
MODERN RELATIVE BYSTANDER TEST	Plaintiff who suffers emotional injury immediately outside of the "target zone" may still recover for her demonstrated harm.	(1) Plaintiff and injured party must be close family relations; (2) Plaintiff must have been present at the scene of the injury; AND (3) Plaintiff must have observed the event causing the victim physical injury.	Emotional distress can be suffered by someone who witnesses an injury of a close relative, even if she is not within the immediate zone of danger.	*A mother who is looking out her window sees her child hit by a negligently driven car can recover for the emotional distress caused by having witnessed the accident even though she was not within the zone of danger.*	Used by modern courts.

Affirmative Defenses to Intentional Torts

An intentional tort is a wrongful act or an infringement of a right leading to a legal liability that was brought about by defendant's intentional conduct. Affirmative defenses may be used to excuse defendant's conduct.

	Defense	Definition	Application	
CONSENT	Express Consent	Written or verbal words that give someone permission to engage in the tortious act.	Express consent can be used as a defense to ALL intentional torts.	
	Implied Consent	Intent can be inferred from the reasonable interpretation of a person's conduct, lack of conduct, the surrounding circumstances or customs.	Implied consent can be used as a defense to ALL intentional torts.	
PROTECTIVE DEFENSES	Self-Defense	The use of reasonable force to prevent the harmful force or offensive bodily contact that a person reasonably believes is being committed against them.	Assault. Battery.	False Imprisonment. Intentional Infliction of Emotional Distress.
	Defense of Others	The use of reasonable force to prevent the harmful force or offensive bodily contact that a person reasonably believes is being committed against another.	Assault. Battery.	False Imprisonment. Intentional Infliction of Emotional Distress.
	Defense of Property	The use of reasonable force to defend a person's land or personal property.	Trespass to Land. Trespass to Chattels.	Conversion
RECAPTURE OF CHATTELS		The use of reasonable force by a property owner to regain possession of personal property taken by another.	Trespass to Chattels.	Conversion.
REENTRY ONTO LAND		The use of reasonable force by a property owner to regain possession of her real property.	Trespass to Land.	
NECESSITY	Public Necessity	The interference with another's land or personal property in an emergency to protect a group of people or community from serious harm.	Trespass to Land. Trespass to Chattels.	Conversion.
	Private Necessity	The interference with another's land or personal property in an emergency to protect people or property.	Trespass to Land. Trespass to Chattels.	Conversion.

Applicability of Consent as a Defense to Intentional Torts

An intentional tort is a wrongful act or an infringement of a right leading to a legal liability that was brought about by defendant's intentional conduct.

Type	Definition	Valid Defense?	Examples
IMPLIED CONSENT	Intent can be inferred from the reasonable interpretation of a person's conduct, lack of conduct, the surrounding circumstances or customs.	✔	*A man asks a woman if he can kiss her and she nods and smiles. Her conduct is sufficient to imply consent.*
EXPRESS CONSENT	Written or verbal words that give someone the authority to engage in the tortious act.	✔	*If a landowner tells her neighbor that the neighbor may cross her property to get to the river, the landowner has expressly consented to the neighbor's use of her property.*
CONSENT AS A MATTER OF LAW	Consent can be implied even if a person is unable to consent where immediate action is necessary to save a person's life, there is no indication the person would not consent, and a reasonable person would consent under the circumstances.	✔	*An unconscious patient is brought into the emergency room after a car accident and surgery is needed to save her life. The surgeon has implied consent to operate.*
ATHLETIC CONSENT	Consent to physical contact customarily engaged in within a particular sport is implied when a person engages in that contact sport.	✔	*During a football game a player tackles an opposing player. Tackling players is recognized as a part of playing the sport. The opposing player has impliedly consented to being tackled by participating in the football game.*
MISTAKEN CONSENT	Consent that would not have been given if the consenter had not been mistaken about a material feature or portion of the transaction.	✔	*Jane allows Sam to go into the pool with her watch because she believes it to be waterproof. Even though the watch was destroyed by Sam, Jane's consent, despite being mistaken, can be used as a defense to a conversion claim.*
CONSENT BY THE INCAPACITATED	Implied or express consent from a person incapable of consenting will not excuse an intentional tortfeasor from liability.	✘	*Consent from a child, a mentally disabled person or an intoxicated person to any intentional tort will not serve as an excusable defense.*

Affirmative Defenses to Intentional Torts: Protection of Self & Others

An intentional tort is a wrongful act or an infringement of a right leading to a legal liability that was brought about by defendant's intentional conduct.

	Definition	Can Deadly Force Be Used?	Is Mistake a Valid Excuse?
SELF-DEFENSE	The use of reasonable force to prevent the harmful force or offensive bodily contact that a person reasonably believes is being committed against them.	✔	Mistakes are allowed so long as defendant's beliefs were reasonable.
DEFENSE OF OTHERS	The use of reasonable force to prevent the harmful force or offensive bodily contact that a person reasonably believes is being committed against another.	✔	To support a claim of defense of another, the individual protected must actually have been in danger. Mistakes are not excusable even where reasonable.
DEFENSE OF PROPERTY	The use of reasonable force to defend a person's land or personal property. Mechanical devices may be employed provided the level of force is no greater than that which is reasonable.	✘	If the mistake is about whether force is necessary, defendants are protected by a reasonable mistake. But if the owner's mistake is about whether a trespasser has a right to be there, the excuse will fail unless the trespasser misled the owner regarding her identification or authorization.

Limitations on the Use of Self-Defense

Self-Defense is the use of reasonable force to prevent the harmful force or offensive bodily contact that a person reasonably believes is being committed against them.

	Rule	Consequences	Examples
DEGREE OF FORCE	The use of force that a person may use in self-defense is that which appears reasonably necessary in that circumstance, for protection against the potential bodily harm. Only that degree of force necessary to prevent the harm may be used.	One who uses excessive force beyond what reasonably appears necessary under the circumstances will be liable for the injuries that ensued as a result of the excessive force.	*Matt punched Jon in the arm. In response, Jon shoots Matt with a gun. Self-defense will not be available as an excuse for Jon's actions since shooting Matt was not reasonably necessary.*
USE BY ASSAILANT	The initial aggressor is not privileged to defend herself against the victim's reasonable use of force in self-defense.	Although the initial aggressor may not assert self-defense against the victim's reasonable use of force in self-defense, if that victim uses deadly force against the aggressor who only used non-deadly force to begin with, the aggressor may defend herself with deadly force.	*Sarah attacked Mariel. In self-defense, Mariel began punching Sarah. If Sarah then grabs a bat to protect herself from Mariel, Sarah will not be able to assert self-defense as a defense for the damages that resulted from her use of the bat.*
RETALIATION	Self-defense is limited to the right to use force to prevent the commission of a tort. Self-defense may never be used if there is no longer a threat of injury.	If the threat of harm or injury has passed, victim will be treated as an assailant if she subsequently initiates a physical altercation with the initial aggressor.	*Kyle attacks Keith in a bar and Keith responds by punching Kyle repeatedly in self-defense. Kyle then leaves the bar. If Keith follows Kyle and attacks him in the parking lot, Keith cannot assert self-defense for the altercation in the parking lot.*
MISTAKE	The use of force in mistaken belief that it was necessary to protect oneself does not violate the availability of the defense.	Courts differ in their application of mistake to self-defense. Some courts have held that victims will be liable for the force mistakenly used unless the assailant was responsible for causing victim's mistake. Other courts have held that victim is liable unless victim exercised the highest degree of care reasonable under the circumstances.	*Lanie points a toy gun directly at Adam's head and tells him that she is going to shoot him if he tries to escape. Not realizing the gun is fake, Adam takes out a real gun and kills Lanie. Most courts will hold that Adam's actions were justified since he reasonably believed he needed to use deadly force in self-defense.*
USE OF DEADLY FORCE	Deadly force may only be used in self-defense where the victim is threatened with death or great bodily harm.	Victim will only be justified for having used deadly force in self-defense in situations where there is an imminent danger of great bodily harm or death, there is no other means of escape and it is the only way to stop the attack.	*Gayle was in her basement when Al came in with a machete. Al cornered her and stabbed her twice. Gayle reasonably feared for her life and was therefore justified in shooting Al to save herself.*
NECESSITY OF RETREAT	Victim need not attempt to escape before using force in self-defense, however, victim must retreat rather than use deadly force if there is a safe way to do so, unless she is attacked in her home or on her property.	If victim uses deadly force instead of retreating when there was a safe way to do so, the defense may be unavailable.	*Sylvia was attacked by her ex-boyfriend Simon who was chasing her with a knife. Simon fell into a ditch while chasing her, providing Sylvia with ample opportunity to escape. Instead, Sylvia shot Simon. Most courts would hold Sylvia's use of deadly force was not justified.*

Strict Tort Liability

In the following situations, liability is automatically imposed upon an actor upon demonstrating (i) causation and (ii) damages.

Strict Liability Situations	Rule	Elements	Examples
ABNORMALLY DANGEROUS ACTIVITIES	Strict liability is imposed upon a person who knowingly engages in abnormally dangerous activities which involve a high degree of risk of serious injury to people or property and which cannot be eliminated by the exercise of reasonable care.	(1) The activity creates a foreseeable and highly significant risk of physical harm even when reasonable care is exercised; AND (2) The activity is not one of common usage.	*Use of explosives.* *Storing or moving hazardous waste.* *Testing rockets.* *Maintenance of a nuclear reactor.*
WORKERS' COMPENSATION	Workers' compensation is a no-fault system, which means that an employee injured while on the job need not demonstrate that her injury was a result of employer negligence. All she has to do is prove is that she was actually injured at work.	(1) Employee injured; (2) The injury occurred on the job; AND (3) Workers' compensation is the sole remedy against the employer.	*An employee that gets into a car accident en route to or from work cannot collect workers' compensation.* *An employee that gets into a car accident while travelling on business can collect workers' compensation.*
WILD OR VICIOUS ANIMALS	Strict liability is imposed upon the owners of a wild animal and upon the owners of domestic animals who know or should have known of the animal's propensity to do an act that might endanger a person's safety or the property of others.	(1) Animal that is wild or known to have dangerous propensities; (2) Causation; AND (3) Damages.	*If a domesticated dog escapes from the yard and bites a neighbor, the dog owner will **not** be strictly liable for the neighbor's injuries provided the dog owner was not on notice of the dog's propensity to bite.* *If the owner knew the dog had a propensity for biting, the owner would be strictly liable for injuries resulting from the dog's bite.* *If owner kept a wolf in his yard that bit the neighbor, the owner would be strictly liable for injuries caused by the wolf irrespective of whether owner has notice of its propensity to bite or not.*
PRODUCTS LIABILITY	Strict liability is imposed upon the manufacturer, retailer or supplier of goods under circumstances in which a defect in their goods causes injury to a purchaser or a bystander.	(1) A person suffers injury or property damage, AND (2) The injury or damage is the result of a dangerously defective product, which was defective in its production, design or safety warning.	*A soda manufacturer is liable for a woman's eye injury caused by the explosion of a soda's cap.*

Products Liability

Product liability imposes liability on manufacturers, distributors, suppliers, and retailers for the injuries their products cause. Plaintiff can recover under a theory of negligence or strict liability.

Types of Claims		Definition	Liability	Available Damages
NEGLIGENCE		When a manufacturer fails to use reasonable care in inspecting, testing or assembling a product's parts or fails to warn of dangers in the product's use.	A manufacturer of a defective product may be found liable if the negligently made product is reasonably certain to place the foreseeable consumer's life and limb in danger when the product is being used in the way in which it was intended or for another reasonably foreseeable use.	Personal injury. Property damages.
STRICT LIABILITY	**Manufacturing Defects**	When there is an anomaly in a mass-produced product that makes it more dangerous.	A manufacturer is automatically liable for any foreseeable injuries that result from its having sold an ordinarily safe product in a defective condition.	Personal injury. Property damages.
	Design Defects	When a whole line of products have a defective design that is unreasonably dangerous.	If there is a reasonable alternative design for the product that is safer, cost-effective and will not impair the utility of the product, a manufacturer will be automatically liable for any foreseeable injuries that result from its defective design.	Personal injury. Property damages.
	Failure to Warn	When there is no warning to a consumer that there is an inherent, non-obvious danger that exists in the product.	A manufacturer is automatically liable if its product is not reasonably safe due to inadequate instructions or a failure to warn a consumer that an inherent, non-obvious danger exists.	Personal injury. Property damages.

Types of Defamation

Defendant makes a statement of or concerning plaintiff, which is harmful to plaintiff's reputation and which is communicated to a third party. Defamation encompasses libel and slander. Libel refers to written or otherwise memorialized defamation, while slander refers to oral defamation.

Type		Definition	Damages	Defenses
LIBEL		A defamatory statement that is written or broadcast in a permanent form.	Reputational injury and damages are presumed and need not be proven.	**Consent:** defendant may prove that she had permission to make the defamatory statement.
SLANDER	**SLANDER**	A defamatory statement that is spoken.	Damages not presumed; plaintiff must demonstrate injury to her reputation, usually by proving economic harm.	**Truth:** in matters of private concern, defendant may prove that the defamatory statement is true.
	SLANDER PER SE	Slander regarding one of the following topics, in which the harm is clear such that damages are presumed: Profession or business, Having committed an immoral crime, Having a loathsome disease, OR Being an unchaste woman.	Reputational injury and damages are presumed and need not be proven.	**Humor:** defendant may prove that the audience believed the statements were made as a joke. **Absolute Privilege:** limited to statements made by government officials acting in their official capacities and communications between spouses. **Qualified Privilege:** limited to statements made in good faith on reasonable belief that they were true, made by someone with a personal or professional interest in the information.

Defamation

Defendant makes a statement of or concerning plaintiff, which is harmful to plaintiff's reputation and which is communicated to a third party. Public figures are believed to have voluntarily thrust themselves into the public eye, thereby consenting to increased public scrutiny.

	Definition	Rule	Fault Required	Damages
PRIVATE PERSON/ PRIVATE CONCERN	An ordinary person.	A non-public person can recover for a defamatory statement made about her without proving fault.	<u>No fault</u> needs to be proven.	Damages presumed and need not be proven by plaintiff.
PRIVATE PERSON/ PUBLIC MATTER	An ordinary person who voluntarily engages in a matter of public controversy (*i.e., a protestor or community activist*).	The individual is subject to the rule for private persons allowing for recovery without fault; except that the private person is treated as a public figure for matters involving a public controversy that is of public concern.	Defamer must have acted at least <u>negligently</u> or with malice as to the statement's truth or falsity.	Damages presumed and need not be proven by plaintiff for matters that are of private concern. Otherwise, damages available if there was actual injury.
PUBLIC FIGURE	A person who has voluntarily gained a sufficient amount of fame which has made her a public figure (*i.e., a movie star or politician*).	A public figurehead may not recover for a defamatory statement made about her without clear and convincing evidence that the defamatory statement was made with malice; intentional or reckless disregard of the truth.	Defamer must have acted with <u>malice</u> by either knowing of the falsity or acting with reckless disregard as to the truth or falsity.	Damages available if there was actual injury.

Determining Whether a Statement Is Defamatory

A defamatory statement is a statement of or concerning plaintiff, which is harmful to plaintiff's reputation and which is published to a third party.

Statements About	Example	Defamatory?	Rule
DEAD PEOPLE	*Marilyn Monroe couldn't sing, she always lip synced.*	✘	Defamatory statements about a deceased person are not actionable.
PARTNERSHIPS & CORPORATIONS	*Don't buy an Apple computer, the company is about to file for bankruptcy.*	✔	Defamatory statements about a company's financial condition, business practices, honesty or morality are actionable.
ALL MEMBERS OF A SMALL GROUP	*Everyone on the treasury committee of the organization steals.*	✔	Defamatory statements referring to everyone in a small group are actionable.
ALL MEMBERS OF A LARGE GROUP	*Everyone who belongs to Alcoholics Anonymous also has drug problems.*	✘	Defamatory statements about all members of a large group are not actionable.
SOME MEMBERS OF A SMALL GROUP	*The dads on the Roslyn Middle School PTA are unemployed.*	✔	Defamatory statements about some members of a small group can be actionable if a reasonable person would consider the statement to be of or concerning the plaintiff.
LOATHSOME DISEASES	*Dave sleeps with a lot of women, it's no surprise he has STDs.*	✔	Defamatory statements about plaintiff having a loathsome disease, such as a venereal disease or leprosy, are considered slander per se and are actionable.
BUSINESS OR PROFESSION	*Hiring Leigh as your assistant is a mistake; she is very disorganized.*	✔	Defamatory statements unfavorably portraying plaintiff's business or professional abilities are considered slander per se and are actionable.
IMMORAL CRIMES	*Craig was fired as the company's accountant because he was caught cheating on his taxes and stealing money.*	✔	Defamatory statements about plaintiff having committed a crime of moral turpitude are considered slander per se and are actionable.
UNCHASTITY	*Michele cheated on her husband.*	✔	Defamatory statements about plaintiff being unchaste are considered slander per se and are actionable.

Invasion to Right of Privacy

The law protects against arbitrary interferences with a person's privacy, family, home or correspondence, and attacks upon honor or reputation.

Type	Definition	Elements	Defenses	Exceptions	Examples
MISAPPRO- PRIATION	Unauthorized use of a person's name or image for another person's commercial advantage.	(1) Use of plaintiff's name or likeness that is protected by the law, (2) For commercial gain or another exploitative purpose, (3) Without plaintiff's consent.	Consent.	News- worthiness exception.	*Sports drink company uses an athlete's image to promote their drink without the athlete's permission.*
INTRUSION	Invasion of a person's private affairs or seclusion in a way that is objectionable to a reasonable person.	(1) Intentional invasion of private affairs of plaintiff without authorization; (2) The invasion would be offensive to a reasonable person; (3) The matter intruded upon is private; AND (4) The intrusion must have caused mental anguish or suffering. ** Does NOT require a publication. **	Consent.	None.	*Eavesdropping. Wiretapping. Spying.*
FALSE LIGHT	Widespread dissemination of a major mis- characterization of a person that would be objectionable to a reasonable person.	(1) Defendant widely published the information (not to just a single person, as in defamation), (2) The publication identifies plaintiff, (3) It places plaintiff in a way that would be highly offensive to a reasonable person, AND (4) Defendant was at fault in publishing the information.	Consent. Truth. Absolute Privilege. Qualified Privilege.	None.	*Plaintiff's photograph of her in a Halloween costume was published as part of an article profiling prostitution in the area. Although the article does not identify plaintiff as being a prostitute, the photograph may be interpreted to suggest that plaintiff is associated with prostitution, thereby raising the possibility of a successful false light publicity claim.*
PUBLIC DISCLOSURE	Widespread dissemination of private information that would be objectionable to a reasonable person.	(1) A publication to the general public absent any waiver or privilege; (2) Of private matters; (3) In which the public has no legitimate concern; AND (4) Such as to bring humiliation or shame to a person of ordinary sensibilities.	Consent. Truth. Absolute Privilege. Qualified Privilege.	News- worthiness exception.	*Financial information. Health care information.*

Nuisance

An unreasonable interference that interferes with a person's use or possession of land. Nuisances are most commonly in the form of disturbing noises, objectionable odors, smoke or other kinds of pollution.

Standard	Definition	Interference With	Example	Remedies	Defenses
PRIVATE NUISANCE	An unreasonable, substantial interference with the use or enjoyment of another's property, without an actual trespass onto the property.	Individual property owner.	*A dry cleaner is on the first floor of a residential apartment building. It emits foul odors and noxious gases that are released into the apartments above. The residents are always coughing and cannot use their balconies. The residents would have a private nuisance claim against the dry cleaner for the unreasonable and substantial interference with their use and enjoyment of their apartments.*	Abatement of the nuisance. Monetary damages.	**Coming to the Nuisance:** Although defendant may claim that plaintiff "came to the nuisance" by purchasing land next to an existing nuisance, plaintiff is entitled to the reasonable use and enjoyment of her land the same as someone who owned the property before the nuisance began. However, the defense may be considered in deter-mining the reasonableness of defendant's acts. **Zoning and Licenses:** Defendant may argue that zoning laws or legislative licenses permit her actions, however this defense will not excuse defendant from liability if her acts are otherwise an unreasonable interference.
PUBLIC NUISANCE	An unreasonable act or omission that obstructs, damages or interferes with a right common to the general public.	Community.	*A new chemical production factory opened in town. Emissions from the factory created air pollution and smog in the town, causing the town residents to have to wear face masks when being outdoors for extended periods of time. The town would have a public nuisance claim against the factory since the factory is unreasonably interfering with the residents' use and enjoyment of their land.*	Criminal Sentence. Fine. Injunction. Abatement of the nuisance. Monetary Damages only available for a person who suffers harm greater than that suffered by the community.	

Intentional Interference with Business Relations

The following are causes of action for damages as a result of defendant's intentional interference with plaintiff's contractual or business relationships.

	Definition	Defenses	Example
INJURIOUS FALSEHOOD	Defendant makes statements about plaintiff's goods or business with recklessness as to its truth, or with knowledge that it is false or misleading, which is communicated to a third party and results in actual damages to plaintiff.	**Truth:** defendant's statement was true. **Fair Competition:** defendant's statement was a fair way of pursuing competition (*i.e., puffery, comparison of her product v. plaintiff's*).	*At a toy convention, the owner of Playtime Toys announced that her rival, American Toy Co., used child labor to build toys. As a result, toy stores stopped carrying American Toy Co. toys. If American Toy Co. does not use child labor to build its toys, it may have a claim against Playtime Toys for its lost sales as a result of Playtime's intentional, false statement.*
INTERFERENCE WITH EXISTING CONTRACTS	Although plaintiff has a contract with a third party, defendant knowingly and maliciously induces the third party to break the contract, resulting in actual damages to plaintiff.	**Privilege:** defendant's acts may be privileged if they arose out of defendant trying to obtain business for herself or to protect her own professional interests.	*Boom Nightclub contracts with DJ Spin to perform on Halloween, one of its biggest nights of the year. Smash Club, a competing nightclub, induces DJ Spin to perform there on Halloween instead. Boom Nightclub may be able to recover against Smash Club for interference with its contracts with DJ Spin.*
INTERFERENCE WITH BUSINESS EXPECTANCY	Defendant intentionally and improperly interfered with plaintiff's probable, future contractual relations or employment opportunities for which plaintiff has a reasonable expectation of financial gain.	**Privilege:** defendant's acts may be privileged if they arose out of defendant trying to obtain business for herself or to protect her own professional interests.	*Rival architects Natalie and Tara bid to build a new office building. Knowing that Tara had worked with the landowner numerous times before and was more likely to have her bid accepted and that the landowner was an animal rights activist, Natalie wrote an article about how Tara loves to hunt recreationally. If the article influenced the landowner's decision to pick Natalie, Tara may have a claim.*

Wrongful Institution of Legal Proceedings

	Definition	Elements	Examples
MALICIOUS PROSECUTION	A criminal proceeding intentionally and maliciously instituted or caused to be instituted by defendant for an improper purpose without probable cause.	(1) Institution of a criminal proceeding against plaintiff, (2) Brought maliciously and without probable cause that the claim was justified, (3) Primarily for a reason other than bringing plaintiff to justice, (4) Proceedings ended in favor of plaintiff, (5) Plaintiff suffered damages.	*Jeffrey thinks Stacie stole his iPod, but he can't prove it. To get revenge on Stacie for being a thief, Jeffrey tells police that he witnessed Stacie robbing a local convenience store so that Stacie would be arrested and prosecuted.*
WRONGFUL INSTITUTION OF CIVIL PROCEEDINGS	A civil lawsuit intentionally and maliciously instituted without a good faith purpose.	(1) Institution of a civil proceeding against plaintiff, (2) Brought maliciously and without a good faith basis that the claim was justified, (3) For a reason other than succeeding on the merits of the claim, (4) Proceedings ended in favor of plaintiff, (5) Plaintiff suffered actual damages.	*Lauryn brought a frivolous sexual harassment claim against her boss at BankCorp, knowing that BankCorp would never allow such a case to go trial because it would not want the bad publicity before its scheduled merger with WorldBankCo. Since the proceedings were brought solely for the purpose of extorting a settlement, BankCorp may have a claim for wrongful institution of civil proceedings against Lauryn.*
ABUSE OF PROCESS	Intentional misuse of litigation devises, criminal or civil, for a purpose other than that for which the process was intended.	(1) Intentional misuse of process, (2) To accomplish a motive other than seeking justice.	*Bari properly brings a lawsuit against Jeff for defamation, but then uses her right of subpoena to harass Jeff because she is so angry about what he said about her, instead of as a means of obtaining his testimony. Bari's actions are an abuse of process.*

Vicarious Liability

Vicarious Liability (aka Respondeat Superior) is a doctrine that holds one party liable for another's actions based upon their relationship.

Relationship		Imputed Liability	Rule
Partner.	Partner.	✔	Each member of a partnership is vicariously liable for the tortious conduct of the others taken within the scope of partnership business.
Employer.	Employee.	✔	An employer is vicariously liable for the tortious conduct of an employee, unless the employee's act was not within the scope of employment.
Employer.	Independent Contractor.	✘	An employer is not vicariously liable for the tortious conduct of an independent contractor, unless the independent contractor is engaged in an inherently dangerous activity or the independent contractor's duty is to keep the premises safe for customers.
Master.	Servant.	✔	A master is vicariously liable for the tortuous conduct of her servant.
Automobile Driver.	Car Owner.	✘	An automobile owner is not vicariously liable for the tortious conduct of another person driving her car, unless imposed by statute.
Husband.	Wife.	✘	A husband is not vicariously liable for the tortious conduct of his wife, and a wife is not vicariously liable for the tortious conduct of her husband.
Parent.	Child.	✘	A parent is not vicariously liable for the tortious conduct of a child, but liability in negligence may be imposed upon the parents themselves for allowing a child to do something dangerous.
Bailor.	Bailee.	✘	A bailor is not vicariously liable for the tortious conduct of her bailee, but liability in negligence may be imposed upon the bailor for entrusting the bailee with the object.
Tavern Keeper.	Patron.	✘	No liability is imposed upon vendors of alcohol for injuries resulting from the patron's intoxication, unless imposed by a state's Dram Shop Act which allows a third party injured by the patron's intoxicated acts to sue the tavern keeper.